Connected for All Time
Book Two

Healing Grief After Infant Loss
A Journey of Spiritual Awakening

Sharon J. Wesch, Ph.D.

Copyright © 2023 by Sharon J. Wesch, Ph.D.
ISBN 978-0-9839173-1-1
Second Printing

Cover Artwork: Carolyn Utigard Thomas (www.utigard.com)
Layout and design: Kouba Graphics, Inc. (www.koubagraphics.com)

10 9 8 7 6 5 4 3 2

Dedication

This book is dedicated to all the
spirit babies in these stories.
They bring powerful medicine
for healing grief.

Angel's Lullaby

By Carolyn Utigard Thomas
(www.utigard.com)

This guardian angel embraces an infant
in everlasting peace and safety.
Be comforted by her loving gaze
and listen for her quiet lullaby.

Table of Contents

Introduction

My soul called for me to write these stories of healing grief when a beloved baby crosses over. Over the past ten years this calling has evolved into two books, *Connected for All Time: Book One* and *Connected for All Time: Book Two*. It might be helpful, but certainly not necessary, to read *Book One* first because it contains introductory information about the healing powers of the spirit babies and the use of Radiant Heart Healing to release the energy of grief and replace it with the energy of love.

Both of these books are part of my mission—the work my soul came to earth to accomplish. As with any mission, Spirit provided all the assistance I needed through direct guidance from my own soul, my spirit guides, my angels, Mother Mary, and a collective of all the spirit babies in both books. I believe these spirit babies provided the many synchronistic meetings that brought each healing story to my attention. They also guided me as I sat at my computer. It seems there was a "baby on my shoulder" the entire time I was writing both the stories and the grief theory. My heart is filled with deep gratitude for all this spiritual assistance.

What You'll Find in This Book

This book contains stories of families who have gone through the experience of losing a beloved infant and have used this crisis as the doorway to spiritual awakening. As you will see, healing grief after the loss of an infant is a journey—not just a single moment in time. For each family this journey is guided by the spirit of their beloved infant as well as other spiritual guides and angels. Therefore, each journey is unique, just as we are each unique souls. Some parents have their awakening within days of losing their infant, while others take far longer. One mother does not recognize her connection to her spirit baby for forty years; during this momentous event her grief is instantly healed. All of these stories send a common message: *After the death of an infant, it is possible to completely free yourself from suffering and transform your grief into joy. The key is learning to release your human pain and then open your heart to the joy of connecting with your spirit baby.*

This book provides an amazing testimony to the many benefits of seeking deep, spiritual healing after the death of an infant. All of the stories send this message: *The death of every baby has meaning and purpose.* When you understand the spiritual purpose of your baby's short time on earth, you will find the answer to these burning questions: *Why, God? Why did my baby come and leave so quickly? What spiritual lessons am I to learn from this tragedy?*

With these healing stories of connection, the spirit babies have also invited you, the reader, on a journey of awakening. They want you to know these spiritual truths:

- Death is not the end of life, and you can create an on-going spiritual relationship with your baby in heaven through the miracle of spirit communication.

- Yearning for a heart connection with your beloved spirit baby is meant to be the catalyst for your own spiritual transformation.

- The eternal soul love shared between you and your spirit baby is the bridge for crossing the chasm between the physical world and the spiritual world.

- Your connection to your beloved spirit baby is a stepping-stone for connecting to the spirit world in general—your angels, your spirit guides, the energy of your own soul, and the God-energy.

It is my sincere hope that these books will inspire you to begin your own journey of spiritual awakening. Healing grief after the loss of your beloved infant requires soul growth and raising your own vibratory frequency. This soul growth is the very reason you came to earth. May you enjoy creating your own unique journey.

Note from the Author:

As you read the stories in this book, you will find numerous references to Radiant Heart Healing. This is a spiritual healing modality that I created in 1984 and now use to assist people who are dealing with grief. Please refer to *Connected for All Time: Book One*, Chapter Eight for a detailed explanation of Radiant Heart Healing.

PREFACE

The Call of Spirit—
Feeling a Pull on My Heart

It's funny, when the phone rings, the person on the other end of the line never says, "Hello, this is destiny calling." And yet, it can be just that. It sometimes takes a while, maybe even years, to understand that this phone call is offering you an opportunity to fulfill your soul purpose—the forgotten promises your soul made before ever coming to earth. Even for those of us who are spiritually awake, we can sometimes be unconscious when Spirit calls. This was certainly the case when my office phone rang one quiet August morning.

In response to my hello, a voice said, "This is Sandy. Can you pray for my new grandbaby? His name is Cole and he's in the neonatal intensive care unit. I'm so worried." Sandy was a counselor in Wisconsin who had been in training with me for the previous three years. Her heartache coming over the phone wires touched me to the core. I offered to call my network of healers to begin prayer chains for Baby Cole. We finished the conversation with Sandy feeling a bit uplifted knowing healers all over the country would be praying for her grandson.

The next few days I couldn't stop thinking about Baby Cole—he was on my mind and in my heart. On the fourth day, I called Sandy for a progress report; Baby Cole was doing worse and was now on a heart-lung machine. Oddly, my chest actually hurt with this news and I began to feel this peculiar, yet undeniable, pulling sensation around my heart. I heard myself saying, "Do you want me to come?" Without hesitation, Sandy answered, "Yes, of course." I had no clue why I was volunteering and no plan about what to do for a baby in intensive care—I was simply responding to the energetic pull on my heart.

Volunteering to assist this family and their critically ill baby turned out to be one of those defining moments in my life; this choice opened yet another new career path—a focus on healing grief after the loss of an infant. The mystical experiences surrounding Baby Cole are amazing; I felt both humbled and blessed to receive brief glimpses of heaven right here on earth as Grandma Sandy and I sent healing energy into Cole's tiny baby body while he lay unconscious in the hospital.

Baby Cole lived twelve days in the Neonatal Intensive Care Unit (NICU, pronounced "nick-you") before making his transition to the other side. This powerful soul was able to pierce the veil between the two worlds within hours and make a connection with his loved ones here on earth. Over the next three years, I had the privilege of guiding several members of Cole's family as they created a spiritual solution to their grief. I also began to document the profound spiritual wisdom sent by this magnificent soul we knew as Baby Cole. Recording that wisdom was the birthing of *Connected for All Time: Book One* and *Book Two.*

Another Moment of Destiny Calling

Five years after Cole's death, I was feeling very stuck in the process of writing these books about healing grief after the death of an infant. The stories were flowing to me effortlessly, yet I couldn't seem to find the unifying thread to knit them together. While on vacation in Sedona, Arizona, I had one of those synchronistic encounters that could only have been arranged by Spirit. As I finished meditating on Bell Rock one morning, I met Wachan, an Inca medicine man from Peru. This holy man handed me the key to weaving these stories together when he explained the Inca cultural beliefs about spirit babies. It was truly a moment of destiny calling! (You can read the expanded version of this encounter in Chapter One of *Connected for All Time: Book One.*) With great humility, this awesome being spoke to me in broken English.

> *My name is Wachan. I am an Inca medicine man. This is my wife who plays the flute. Our home is in Peru near the famous mountain called Machu Pichu (Ma-choo Pee-choo). We are living here in Sedona for now and teaching others about our ways. I must tell you about the spirit babies in the Inca traditions.*
>
> *We believe spirit babies surround Pachatusan (Pa-cha-too-san), a sacred mountain in Peru not far from Machu Pichu. This sacred place is our burial ground for babies. Since time began all Incas make the trek to Pachatusan when death comes to a baby. It's an ancient Inca tradition.*
>
> *The spirits of these babies form a big circle high in the sky all around the mountain. When you go there and listen quietly, you can hear their beautiful music. The sound is so pure it sounds like*

the angels are singing. Just the baby spirits live there; that's why the sound is so pure. We believe the spirits of the babies bring us our purity—they bring us light. And so we call them "the keepers of purity."

If you go to the mountain at sunset, you can hear the babies singing their beautiful music. I take many visitors there. I ask them to listen and tell me what they hear. They tell me, "It sounds like the wind is singing." Then I tell them of the babies who live there.

Pachatusan is also called "the medicine man mountain." All Inca healers (medicine men) go there for their spiritual training. When you come back from the mountain you are ready to work. That is the tradition.

The Inca people also go to this sacred place for healing if they are sick in mind, body, or spirit. The healing energy of the spirit babies at Pachatusan is powerful medicine. We Incas want the world to know of the healing power of the spirit babies.

So I give you these words as a gift for your book.

And I give you my blessings.

Meeting this holy man and receiving his message about the Inca cultural beliefs gave me the inspiration to emphasize the idea that spirit babies really do bring healing to their grieving loved ones. As I stated in *Book One*, in our modern American culture we have no such tradition. However, you will see as you read these fascinating stories that we are no different from the ancient Incas. Indeed, both *Connected for All Time: Book One* and *Book Two* are filled with story after story showing that, even now, in twenty-first-century America, when a beloved baby goes to heaven, the spirit of that baby remains connected to the family and other loved ones here on earth. The force that connects them is soul love—the powerful medicine that heals grief.

This book is about the healing power of the spirit babies.
They heal grief through connection.

CHAPTER ONE

Love Is Stronger Than Death

Cole taught me that unconditional love is about loving
when you don't get anything back.
—*Cole's Grandpa Dan*

Gary and Danita are a young Midwestern couple who work together in their own construction business. They decided it was time to start a family and were overjoyed when Danita discovered she was pregnant. Life seemed to be unfolding exactly the way they planned; their business was quite successful, they were building a new home, and their hopes and dreams of creating a family were fulfilled. Life was indeed quite blissful.

But their bliss evaporated as their wonderful plan was replaced by an unexpected turn of events. Danita was ten days past her due date when her doctor advised her to check into the hospital to be induced. The labor and delivery were extremely long with one crisis after another until Cole was delivered by emergency C-section. Both Danita and the baby came close to dying several times during the process. Cole was born weighing ten pounds nine ounces and was perfectly formed; he just couldn't breathe.

Cole was in crisis because during the long labor he swallowed his own fecal material, and as a result, was unable to breathe on his own. He was rushed to a NICU, put on a heart-lung machine, placed in a drug-induced coma and hooked up to IVs, tubes, and monitors. The entire family was worried that he was in pain and suffering from procedures that were medically necessary to save his life. Despite heroic efforts, Cole lived only twelve days.

Cole Generates Love

Cole generated great love during his very short life. It was amazing that such a little baby could touch so many hearts and inspire so much affection. Cole, who couldn't talk, smile or even make eye contact, somehow opened the hearts of all his caretakers. Everyone on the hospital staff fell in love with Cole. Indeed, the doctors, nurses, and other support people took Cole into their hearts and had to deal with their own grief when he died. The entire neonatal intensive care staff was openly crying when Cole made his transition. For whatever reasons, Cole held an energy that drew people to him. He was like a magnet for love.

Danita, Gary, and Cole were enveloped in the love that poured out from family, friends, and neighbors. Cole's grandparents, aunts, uncles, and cousins also received cards, flowers, and other expressions of support. Love even poured in from strangers who had joined prayer chains across the country.

Danita's Angel Dreams

If I were to use just one word to paint a picture of Danita, it would be "strong." She possesses physical strength, a powerful personality, and an inner fortitude that helped her through the worst tragedy of her life—the death of her infant son.

Tall and blonde, Danita stands out in a crowd and has an air of statuesque beauty. Yet she certainly doesn't rely on this beauty; she knows what she wants in life and is willing to work for it. This young woman is a real go-getter! Danita has a talent for being very organized, setting goals, visualizing the outcome she wants, and persisting until she manifests her heart's desire. She has used these talents to manage the construction business, where she and her husband work as equal partners; she runs the office while he manages the workers at the construction sites.

In addition, Danita has a very feminine side to her personality: she is generous of heart, a very loyal friend, kind to older people, and enthusiastic about creating a family. She loves babies and had always planned to have children of her own.

Immediately after Cole's death, Danita began to have a very vivid, recurring dream of her son. She believed the dreams were an answer to her prayers. Each night she would lie in bed repeating this prayer over and over, like a mantra until she fell asleep: "Please, Cole, send me some kind of sign. I need to know that you're okay. I need to know that you are not still suffering." Danita described the dream in these words:

> *Now don't laugh. This is just what I saw in my dream. Cole was flying around with white angel wings attached to his back. He was always buck-naked! [Laughing] He looked like one of those chubby little cherubs. And he would be flying around with lots of other little babies with white angel wings. They were all naked. Of course, I love naked babies! And they were all giggling and having so much*

fun together. He never says anything, but he is always giggling. Each time the dream is the same.

In the beginning, I had this dream every other night. It's been eighteen months since Cole died, and I still have the same dream, maybe once a month.

Danita usually felt great relief each morning when she awoke and remembered seeing her son. She would wake up peaceful, like she had slept for twenty hours. The vision of Cole flying around with other little babies was her confirmation that he was okay. Seeing him happy and giggling gave her a clear message that he was no longer suffering. She could now think of him as an angel and know he was safe in heaven.

However, the feeling of relief did not last long; after the dream, Danita's heart-wrenching grief would return and wash over her again. She thought she was doing something wrong because the grief kept coming back. Danita eventually learned that this was a normal process for people who have lost a loved one. Danita described her fluctuating emotions.

My grief seemed to come in waves. In the beginning the waves were so strong, they almost knocked me right off my feet. Gradually the waves got less intense and spaced further apart. But they still came when I least expected them.

Cole Sends a Sign

In addition to the dreams, several months after Cole's transition, he sent another sign to his mother. When Danita talked about this magical moment, a beautiful glow came over her face.

It was several months after Cole's death, and I was still crying every day. I was feeling utterly devastated. In between the angel dreams, I would sink into despair. Nothing could console my grieving heart.

I was upstairs in my bedroom getting ready to go to work. Suddenly I heard music coming from across the hall in the baby's room. I ran in there, and sure enough, one of Cole's musical toys was moving and playing a little tune.

I knew it was a sign from Cole! There was no other reason for the music to start. This toy has a long string you have to pull to get it to play. Actually, it's pretty hard to pull. How he did that I will never understand, but I know it was him. I was alone in the house, so it

3

couldn't have been anybody else. I stood there by the crib crying tears of joy the whole time the music played.

When I was riding the roller coaster of emotions, I was also going back and forth in my head about Cole. There were days when I fully believed he was alive in heaven. Then there were days when I lost my faith about this. When he played the music, I felt he was saying to me, "Okay, Mom, this is as dramatic as I can be. Wake up! I'm still here." This event certainly did erase my doubts and helped me know that Cole is still alive and able to send me a message.

Both the recurring dream and the musical message brought great comfort to Danita. She saw them as evidence that Cole's spirit was alive and communicating with her from heaven. Even though she desperately wanted him to be living here on earth, she could take comfort that his spirit existed and was happy in heaven.

"Time Heals" Is a Myth

I first interviewed Danita twenty months after Cole's death. She talked about her devastating grief and all the innovative techniques she used to keep moving forward with her life. Danita seemed wise beyond her years as she talked about dealing with her heartache.

Once I got over crying on a constant basis, I thought about what I wanted to do. Then I made goals and started achieving them. I made a decision to concentrate on the positive things that came as a result of Cole's birth and death. I wouldn't let myself dwell on the negatives. There are a lot of good things in my life. I chose to focus on these good things. I can't let death take over my life. It could absolutely eat me up.

Danita's positive attitude was quite extraordinary. Making a conscious choice to focus on the positive was the key component for healing her deep grief after losing Cole. It's not an easy task to remain positive during a crisis, but it is an essential factor of any healing process. Danita understood that while she did not have control over what happened to Cole, she did have command of her thoughts.

This wise young woman seemed to talk about deep philosophical truths in a very nonchalant way. In the midst of our conversation about healing grief, she stated this elegant pearl of wisdom:

"There's an old saying, 'Time heals all wounds.' I think that's a myth. It's what you DO with your time. It's what you focus on during the time."

The Circles of Love Continue

Danita described how her friends continued to send love and support long after Cole's funeral.

My greatest fear is that people will forget Cole. I have this huge anxiety about this issue. My best friend sends me a card on Cole's birthday and another card on his death day. I really appreciate this gesture. Each year, the love I feel from her helps turn a sad day into a blessed day.

The mail delivery was a time I looked forward to each day right after Cole died. We received over two hundred cards, and I loved getting each one. I even made a scrapbook so I could keep them forever. It was devastating when the cards stopped coming. I must say I started asking, "Did people forget?" Then out of the blue, my friend Cheryl sent twelve roses for the twelve days Cole was here with us. I felt so loved.

Danita also learned to generate self-love by being kinder to herself. She let go of some of her own rules about always appearing perfect.

One thing I learned from this experience with Cole is that life is too short to be concerned with minor details. I used to be all uptight about how I looked each time I went out of the house. Now I say, "Who cares what I look like going to the grocery store?" If my husband calls to invite me out for dinner, I just go with the flow and say yes. I don't want to miss an opportunity to enjoy his company. I used to have all these excuses—I have to wash my hair, I have too much to do. Now, I just say yes.

Interacting With Friends

Danita found that people often don't have a clue about what to say to grieving parents. Some of the worst comments were: "You can always have another child," "It's probably better this way," and "He's in a better place." Her thought in response to this was, "The best place for a baby is with his mommy!" She gradually came to understand that most people have not been through the tragedy of losing a baby and therefore don't know what to say.

We had so many friends who came to do things like mow the lawn and bring food. One couple would call and say, "We are bringing dinner, so take a nap for the afternoon." Others would come to just be with Gary and me—we didn't have to talk about anything

> *important. They did this routinely for the first two months after Cole died.*

Danita moves through the world with her outgoing personality up front for everyone to see. You always know where you stand with Danita because she says it like it is. Here are her comments about friends.

> *We have come to appreciate spending time with genuine people who can be real. I tell all my friends, "The death of a child will change your address book forever." We have erased some people from our book, and we have added some who we didn't know well but came to value because they just kept reaching out to help.*

Many people spontaneously offered, "Call me if you need anything." Danita didn't find this vague statement helpful. When Danita knows a friend is going through grief, she makes the phone call and volunteers to help rather than waiting for them to ask. She says, "The reality is that people in grief won't call. They do need help, but they won't ask."

The circles of love continued to grow, rippling out into the world. Danita's experience of grieving awakened a newfound level of empathy and compassion in her heart, and led her to more ways of being helpful and supportive to others. Danita said:

> *I feel like Cole is guiding me to be more loving by giving more of myself to others. I look for ways to help, like baby-sitting for my brother's wife while he is serving in Kuwait, and doing extra special things for my friends on their birthdays. It has to be something more than giving money to charities.*

> *Also, Gary and I are closer than ever. We look at the world in a different way. We take nothing for granted. I know he could be gone tomorrow, and I appreciate that we have each other today.*

A Father's Grief

Cole's father, Gary, is a mosaic of opposites. He is the perfect partner for Danita because he balances her strength: he is gentle of heart, sensitive, and caring. He's also very astute, extremely private and a man's man who loves sports like fishing and hunting. Gary has a great sense of pride about the life he has created working side-by-side with Danita, his wife and business partner.

Gary was overcome with grief when his son died. He was only thirty-three years old at the time and had not experienced losing someone he loved. He described his reaction:

I kept a very optimistic point of view the whole time Cole was in the hospital. Those twelve days in the NICU were incredibly stressful, but I truly believed he would come through this bad time and be okay. It was a big shock when Cole died.

The whole first week after he died was the worst week of my life. I cried a lot then—more than I ever knew I could. The pain was absolutely excruciating. In fact, I couldn't eat or sleep for about two weeks.

Gary was not the type of person to open his heart and talk to strangers. He tried going to a support group for infant loss, but he was too uncomfortable to return. Gary found his own way to release the agonizing pain. He said:

Just being able to talk to friends and family gave me some kind of release. Actually, talking with my wife, Danita, was my greatest outlet. She was my soundingboard and my best listener. I could cry and pour out my heart to her.

After Danita, the people I found most helpful were those who had also lost a baby or a child. They seemed more sensitive, and I could open up and talk to them. It was surprising to find out how many of our acquaintances had lost a baby. There were at least six families who shared their stories with us. Talking to them helped me a lot.

It's been almost two years now, and I think I'm mostly over my grief. There are some memories that still make me cry. Usually I can talk about Cole without crying; in the early days, I couldn't do that. Every time I visit his grave I still cry—and I think that's okay.

New Life Brings Hope

At the time of our first interview, Danita was pregnant again, and this second baby was due the same week as Cole's birth two years earlier. She said:

When strangers notice that I'm pregnant, they often ask, "Is this your first child?" At first, that question caused me great pain, and I didn't know what to say. Now I answer, "It's our second; our first child is in heaven." I feel comfortable with that.

From the beginning, I asked myself the question, "What's going to pull me out of this funk?" Gary and I both decided that having another baby would be crucial to feeling better. You just can't make a child appear on demand, and it took us fourteen months to get

*pregnant again. Knowing we are having another child has helped
our grief tremendously. This baby certainly won't replace Cole or
erase the painful memories, but we are very excited to be moving
on with our dream of starting our family.*

It would be very natural to have many fears about the well-being of this new
baby. Without coaching from a professional, Danita used visualizations to
keep her thoughts positive and her fears at bay.

*I have a one hundred percent belief that this baby is going to be
okay; consequently, I have no fear. I'm getting a healthy infant this
time around, and I know what sheer joy can come from that. Every
day I visualize delivering a healthy baby. I see myself holding this
new little one right next to my heart and surrounding him or her
with so much love. I concentrate on feeling all the joy and love
when this baby is born.*

*This time I know the kind of love I can feel for our baby. It's an
unexplainable love that's so deep it's hard to put into words. I know
I felt unconditional love for Cole, and I feel that same kind of love
for this infant that's growing within me. The whole idea of creating
a baby is such a miracle!*

Danita was a master at creating effective visualizations for healing her
fears. Notice how she concentrated on feeling love and joy while imaging
a healthy baby. The energy of feeling strong, positive emotions created a
powerful, magnetic force vital to attracting her heart's desire.

Danita's Spiritual Reading With a Medium

At the end of our first interview, I suggested to Danita that she might find
it helpful to have a session with a spiritual medium, and she seemed open
to this idea. I recommended a woman I'd been working with for several
years. I knew she was authentic and had a gift for communicating with
deceased loved ones—including babies who were miscarried or stillborn.
I assured Danita that the medium would have no information about her life
or her desires for the reading. I also told her that, while there are never any
guarantees that specific spirits will come through, she might get a message
from Cole.

Hoping to hear from her son, Danita made an appointment for the next
month. Like most people, she didn't know what to expect. She felt quite
anxious because a friend made negative remarks about spiritual mediums;
however, Danita was very excited about the possibility of receiving

reassurance about Cole's safety and happiness. Here are some of the important messages from this reading.

Medium: *The Virgin Mary is here. She comes whenever there has been a child lost. So I think you lost a child. This child says he knew that you loved him, and all is not lost. He really needed to be with you and no one else. If you have animals, these animals are going to be able to see this child because his energy is so strong around you.*

What's with the empty cradle? You keep looking in this empty cradle in your mind. You are so worried and so concerned. You are not letting people know this.

The boy that's been talking from the other side is your son. He comes as a small boy, but he also shows himself as a teenager about nineteen years old. He's very handsome.

He wants me to tell you that his mission here was a test of strength. He needed to test his strength. His purpose was to bring the family together, not apart. He wants to thank you. It was a mission that he was supposed to fulfill.

He felt your love for him. He feels it every day. He tells me to tell you that he loves you. And he's sorry. He saw the opportunity to come in, and he just jumped right in. That's how much he wanted to be with you. He's talking about Wednesday. Do you understand what happened on Wednesday with him?

Danita: *Yes. Cole died on a Wednesday.*

Medium: *Are you pregnant? Are you going to have another baby?*

Danita: *Yes.*

Medium: *He's very excited about this. Who's Thomas? Your child is talking about a Thomas. How old is Thomas?*

Danita: *Thomas is my nephew. He's five.*

Medium: *I think your son who crossed over is very connected to Thomas. I think Thomas was able to communicate with your son when he crossed over. I would love to talk to Thomas and see what he says about this. There's something in your family line that's very strong between these children.*

It could be that the spirit of the child you are carrying is inside already. Sometimes the spirit enters at the moment of conception.

Others times they come in at the time the baby quickens—you know, when the mother first feels the baby move. And sometimes they wait until the last minute to come in.

I can tell you that the child that you lost lived the whole experience. He came in immediately. I have to tell you that the child isn't lost. He has always been with you. It was a joy for him to be carried by you, to have you give birth, and to have you as a mother. He chose you.

There was a greater message here by him crossing over. It was greater than you can ever imagine. It seemed so unfair on many levels, but it was part of his purpose. It was his divine plan. And from his birth came something very important. It's hard because you want to hold your child in your arms and just love him and see him raised. But he did something that was incredible.

You had to be a very strong spirit to accept that responsibility and to accept the challenge. It's not like he decided to do this against your will. Before you were even born, you sat down with him and said, "Okay, this is what's going to happen here." And then you forgot. The love you both had for each other was so great that you both said, "We can do this together." And the love continues on. And one day you are going to see this child face-to-face, and you are going to know that you did the best that you could possibly do. And you are going to know that it was all in divine hands.

Your son is a very strong spirit. He is a very valiant soul. I hope you recognize that. He had a lot of courage. He had so much love that he wanted to share with everyone in that short amount of time that he existed. He's a very empathetic child. Every time he sees you cry, he cries with you. You would enjoy seeing him the way I see him now. He's like a stud—he looks good. [Laughing]

A trauma happened to you that was so great that just getting up took a lot of courage. It gave you an opportunity to meet new people and make new friends. It wasn't easy. Emotionally it took a great amount of strength on your part to keep moving forward. It was like a little butterfly whose wing has been torn. You are still going through the process of letting go. Moving forward has to do with the process of letting go. You lost someone and it's hard. When you finally let go, there is a feeling of peace and celebration, knowing that everything happened the way it did for a reason.

A Certain Kind of Honor

Danita and I met several weeks after this reading, and she reported this amazing shift in her beliefs about her relationship with Cole.

After the session, I felt uplifted and almost had a sense of being privileged that my son died. I know this must sound very weird. I felt like powers way beyond our earthly existence chose me to assist Cole with his purpose. They chose me because they knew I was capable of getting through it, learning from the experience, and surviving it with more comprehension of what life is all about. That to me is a certain kind of honor.

Cole's Greater Message

After listening to the transcript, I asked Danita to explain what the medium meant when she said, "There was a greater message by Cole crossing over. It was greater than you can ever imagine." Danita responded.

Cole's greater message is definitely about love. He taught Gary and me so much about love. I never fully understood love until I had Cole and then lost him. I thought I knew everything, and then I realized I really had no clue.

A baby you love can be taken away from you in an instant. It doesn't matter if you are good or bad, rich or poor, attending church or not. And I found I could still love my baby even though he wasn't here for me to hold or touch or kiss. Loving Cole's spirit really did stretch my heart. This is new for me.

Thomas and Cole

Cole's cousin, Thomas, is a real boy's boy with an abundance of jumping, darting energy. He's always on the move and can usually be found doing some sort of rough-and-tumble antics. His unbridled exuberance fills up whatever room he occupies! The medium was absolutely correct about Thomas being able to communicate with his cousin Cole, who died when Thomas was three years old.

Danita and other family members have numerous stories demonstrating that the two boys seem, even now, to have ongoing conversations. Thomas doesn't seem to notice that he and his cousin are worlds apart, Thomas in the physical world and Cole in the spirit world. Danita reported:

On Mother's Day, Thomas gave me a flowerpot that he had hand-painted. It had a super cute flower in it. Thomas said to me, "Baby Cole wanted to give this to you himself. But he's not here, so I did."

Another time I was babysitting for Thomas, and he announced, "This baby in your tummy is not going to die, Aunt Danita. I know. Cole told me."

Another time I asked Thomas, "How do you know so much?" He responded, "I talked to Baby Cole the other day. He telled me."

One day Thomas was riding home from daycare with his mother, Kim. He was sitting in the front seat right next to Kim when he started making some really weird sounds, as if he were carrying on a conversation with somebody. It seemed to Kim that he was speaking some kind of strange language. Kim asked, "Thomas, what do you want? What are you saying?" Thomas shook his head and didn't answer his mother. Kim responded, "Thomas, you're scaring me. Please stop talking like that." Then Thomas announced, "Mommy, be quiet! I'm talking to Baby Cole."

Kim considered this very strange behavior and was quite concerned that something was seriously amiss with her son. Kim shared her concerns with her stepmother, Sandy, who reassured her, saying: "It's nothing to worry about. Thomas is just very connected to Cole. Little children are closer to the spirit world, and they have no barriers between our world and heaven."

The Transformation of Grandpa Dan

Danita's father is known in the family as Grandpa Dan. He revels in his role of grandfather, and some of his happiest moments are those he shares with his grandchildren.

Dan is a very traditional guy who flew helicopters in Viet Nam, earns a living working as a sales manager at a grocery chain, and loves playing golf. He constantly reads motivational books to improve himself, his career, and his personal life. He has always been the responsible one— the guy who does it all. However, nothing prepared him for his role as grandfather to a baby in crisis.

In this tragic situation, there were no rules to follow, so Dan had to follow his gut feelings and do whatever his heart called him to do. He felt strongly that Cole should never be left alone, so he volunteered to take the night shift. Through the night, Dan talked to his little grandson as if Cole could hear and understand every word. At bedtime, Dan read children's books to Baby Cole. He was the last member of the family to say good night and the first one to say good morning.

Each night I told him he was beautiful and talked to him about how much I loved him. I would also tell him how much Gary, Danita, and his Grandma Sandy loved him. I called him Little Buddy and had long talks with him. There was nothing I could do medically— all I could do was just be there. So that's what I did.

I made this deep connection with my grandson even though he never made eye contact with me and he never smiled at me. He couldn't give me anything. He lived only twelve days, yet he allowed me to experience a deep, unconditional love. I have never had this feeling for anyone else in my whole life—not my parents, my wife, or my own children. Cole taught me that unconditional love is about loving when you don't get anything back.

At Cole's funeral only three people spoke—Grandpa Dan, Cole's great uncle Larry, and a pediatrician who was a friend of the family. These three strong men with soft hearts wrote poems and read them for the eulogy at the funeral. Nobody organized this. Nobody asked them to be part of the funeral ceremony. Amazingly, they each just did it spontaneously. Dan believes Cole's spirit inspired him to write his poem and helped him get through the delivery without breaking down.

Changes in Grandpa Dan

Grandpa Dan went through his own spiritual transformation because of this baby's twelve-day stay on earth. Dan's emotional experiences with Cole motivated him to think about life in a different way. He began asking questions like, "What's life all about anyway?" He came to the conclusion that Cole taught him about living and loving and what's really important. He realized it was no longer important to be a macho man.

Looking back, I realize Cole's death was a big event in my life. It was like being stripped naked and put out on the deck in the freezing cold. I felt like I was an adult curled up in the fetal position with someone saying to me, "Now, figure it out." So I've been figuring out what life is all about. I keep asking myself, "What are you going to take from this? What are you going to do different?" The answers to these questions keep getting clearer for me.

After Cole's death, I got closer to my wife, my daughter, and her husband. All of us were stripped of our usual barriers. We spent time talking from our hearts. I came out of the closet emotionally and started sharing my feelings with people. It's great to be able to do this.

I even spent time one evening sharing one-on-one with another male friend who had just lost his father. Here we were, two grandpas drinking beer and talking with tears coming down our faces. It was a real moment for me! Cole helped me open to this, and I'm forever grateful. I guess you could say Cole helped me open my heart.

Dan found his relationships evolving to a new level of intimacy. He kept his heart open to all those who experienced this trauma and discovered a fuller love with his family and friends.

My relationship with my daughter, Danita, has changed so much. Going through this grief experience together has knocked down a lot of barriers. We are closer and we have a much more comfortable, open relationship. Now we can cut through the bullshit and get our emotions out on the table rather quickly. I've decided life is just too short to play games.

After Cole's death, I started stopping by Danita's office just to talk. It was a time for just the two of us alone. I'd stay thirty minutes to an hour and just talk. Sometimes we would talk about Cole and cry a bit. Other times we would just hang out and talk about whatever. We had these special times alone that I will always remember. Danita used to say, "Dad, the phone stops ringing when you come. I don't understand how that happens. It can be ringing off the wall before you come, but then it just stops."

I also got closer to Danita's husband, Gary, and his father, Don. Don and I were often together at the hospital while Cole was alive. The whole experience hit us two grandpas pretty hard. It really got us! We hugged each other and cried when Cole died. After going through that experience together, we are different with each other. We talk feelings now; this is something we couldn't do before. I will always remember visiting Gary and Danita the day after Cole's death. Gary hugged me saying, "I love you, man. I love you." It was a moment—two macho men hugging, crying, and expressing love!

Actually, I've changed in all my relationships. I'm able to keep my heart open and talk feelings. I've decided to tell the truth, and I don't bullshit around anymore. When I have negative feedback for my sales reps, I say it in a loving manner. People recognize it's coming from my heart. Sometimes my salespeople try to put up a false front so they will look better. I want them to get through the veneer and be real. I've brought several sales reps to tears sitting in the coffee area of a supermarket. They get real, start talking about their feelings, and then we can make some progress. They know my heart is open, and so they open their hearts. It helps them change and grow.

This former macho man hated to admit he was depressed during his grief experience; however, he finally acknowledged the truth about this to himself.

It's taken me several years to overcome my grief about Cole. Actually, I've gone through two years and six months of mourning. I acted as normal as can be and kept going to work as usual. However, I knew I wasn't quite right. Looking back, I guess I would say I've been depressed. I wasn't the person I promised Cole I would be. I had a lot of new beliefs, but I wasn't putting them into practice. I felt bad about this, but I just couldn't seem to do what I wrote down as my goals. I even wrote in my journal, "I'm three-quartering my way through life."

In these last few months, I have really noticed a change in my demeanor. I think I've gone from seventy-five percent to one hundred and ten percent. I am more engaged with everyone and everything. I'm making decisions and following through in many areas of my life. I'm cutting through the bullshit, excuses, and procrastination and just doing it.

Maybe it was the birth of Danita and Gary's new baby Carson (two years after Cole's death) that allowed me to get out of my semi-funk. I really connected with Carson while resting in my favorite blue leather chair in the family room. I was holding him on my lap and looking into his eyes and precious face and making him smile, laugh, and giggle. We were both engaged with each other. It was beautiful! We were in the moment and truly connecting with each other. It didn't hit me at the time, but that ten minutes with him was really important.

Grandpa Dan Connects to Cole's Spirit

Dan has a strong heart-to-heart connection with Cole's spirit; it is a deep love bond forged during those twelve days at the hospital when Dan's emotional heart cracked wide open. He has Cole's picture on his desk and carries another one in his wallet. He has what he calls "his neat little thing with Cole," which means he prays for Cole each day, talks to him routinely in Spirit, and receives guidance from Cole as he goes about his daily life. Dan totally believes Cole is now a spirit who knows what's happening back here on earth and sends inspiration and love to all the family members.

Grandma Sandy

Sandy, Dan's second wife, loves being a grandmother! She just lights up with an inner glow whenever she spends time with her three step-grandchildren, Thomas, his sister Catherine, and Danita and Gary's new baby, Carson.

My first impression of Sandy was "little but mighty." A real go-getter with a vivacious, outgoing personality and a contagious enthusiasm for life, Sandy is a bundle of energy. She has dramatic, crystal blue eyes—in fact, the biggest blue eyes I've ever seen! The light shining from them is quite magnetic and actually attracts people to her. She also has a heart that expands in response to her desire to make connections with people. With her magnetic eyes and her open heart, Sandy is a very powerful connector.

Sandy is a spiritual healer certified in Radiant Heart Healing. She didn't always believe in spiritual healing; in fact, being a healer was a big shift from her traditional roles of Michigan farm girl, schoolteacher, wife, mother of three boys, stepmother, and step-grandmother. Sandy was working as a weight loss counselor at a holistic center when she was invited to attend one of my professional trainings for Radiant Heart Healing.

During this training, Sandy actually felt the spiritual energy and became aware of the reality beyond what we human beings perceive with our five, ordinary human senses. That day she opened her mind, shifted her belief system, and came to believe in the possibility of spiritual healing. This was three years before Cole's crisis. Little did she know she would put her training to use with a precious baby born to her stepdaughter, Danita.

Sandy Makes Eye Contact With Cole

Dan and Sandy went to the hospital as soon as Danita and Gary called. Dan went upstairs to be with Danita; Sandy went to the NICU. Once Sandy got to the nursery, she couldn't leave Cole by himself. The doctors were keeping Cole sedated with medication so he wouldn't try to breathe on his own; they wanted him to use the ventilator. Sandy described an important moment.

At one point, his nurse walked away to get something. Cole started to move. I ran around to the other side of his bed to better see his face. Cole opened his eyes and looked right at me. I said to him, "You're awake! Grandma loves you."

I looked into his eyes and I saw his soul. It was like I could see into eternity. His soul seemed to go on and on. The depth was incredible! At the same time I heard, "I am an eternal spirit and our connection is everlasting. We will be together always, even until the end of time."

This special connection with Cole gave me faith and courage for the difficult days ahead. Whenever I remember that special time with him, my heart opens with love and warmth. It is a moment I will never forget.

When the nurse heard Cole was awake, she immediately gave him another shot of morphine to return him to an unconscious state. Cole never again opened his eyes during his twelve days here on earth.

There's an old saying, "The eyes are the window to the soul." Indeed, Sandy felt a soul connection with Cole when she made eye contact with him. This deep feeling of connection is called "soul recognition," and it motivated Sandy to do whatever she could to help her grandson. She wanted to make sure she had left no stone unturned, and from the first day, she was dedicated in her efforts. She generated an immense amount of love and healing for Cole through her actions and her requests, and these efforts drew many people into the experience.

The Love Grandma

At some time each day, Sandy stood next to Cole in the NICU and sent healing energy into his tiny chest. He was so little that her hand covered his whole upper torso. She was working with these spiritual healing energies one night when a medical technician named Jake started a conversation with her. He asked, "What do you do when you put your hands on your grandson like that?" Sandy answered, "I'm sending him love and healing energy. I picture the healing energy leaving my hands and moving into his body to help him heal his lungs. Jake responded, "We were all wondering what you were doing." The next night Sandy arrived at the NICU and Jake called out, "It's the Love Grandma! We decided to give you that nickname." Sandy laughed and said, "Thanks, Jake. I will wear that title with pride—the Love Grandma!"

Positive Thoughts and Affirmations

Several days after Cole's birth, Sandy called her sister Linda, who studies metaphysics and understands the power of thought. Sandy discussed some of her fears for Cole. Linda told her sister, "You don't have the luxury of a negative thought. You must hold only positive thoughts about Cole. He is relying on all of you for his strength." Sandy then renewed her efforts to keep her thoughts positive and bring an uplifting energy to Cole.

Sandy's training as a healer taught her the benefits of setting optimistic intentions and using positive affirmations. She wanted Cole to know at every level of his being that he was loved, so she repeated these affirmations to him each day while she sent healing energy into his heart. Sandy understood that even though Cole was in a medically induced coma, his spirit could hear and comprehend each message. She expressed her unconditional love to her grandson with these statements:

> *You are loved.*
>
> *You are wanted.*
>
> *You are worthy.*
>
> *You are valuable.*
>
> *You were born exactly at the right time for you.*
>
> *You have a very special purpose in this world that only you can fulfill.*
>
> *You are a radiant being filled with light and love.*
>
> *You are a precious child of God.*

Cole Responds to Prayers and Affirmations

Grandma Sandy formed a good relationship with Cole's primary doctor and spent time asking him for a lot of detail about Cole's physical needs. After he reviewed the medical options with the family, Sandy would ask, "We are praying for certain outcomes here, so what specifically do we need to ask for?"

At one point, the doctor informed the family that a necessary surgery carried a high risk of excessive bleeding; Cole's life would literally hang in the balance. Before the procedure, Sandy sent healing energy into Cole's heart and repeatedly said to him, "You will have very little bleeding during this surgery."

After the surgery, the doctor said in amazement to Sandy, "It was incredible how little he bled." He had no idea that Sandy had used both affirmations and prayer work with Cole to prevent bleeding. It was a minor victory in the long battle to keep Cole alive. After reading Julie Motz's book *Hands of Life*, Sandy understood that Cole's cells and organs were responding to her words.

A Spirit Assists Cole

Sandy is very intuitive and sometimes has the gift of spiritual vision. On occasion, she gets a very clear image of the spirit world. She was both excited and surprised to see a spirit watching over Cole as he lay unconscious.

> *Every time I visited Cole at the NICU, I would see a spirit sitting at the end of his little bed. The lower part of his body appeared very misty, but I could see his head and face very clearly. It was a young boy wearing a backwards baseball cap and a set of headphones, as if he were listening to music. I knew this was my nephew Matt because that's exactly how he always looked when he was here on earth.*

> *As I left Cole's side, Matt sent me the message, "Don't worry about it, Aunt Sandy. I'm watching out for Cole." Thereafter, when I left the hospital I would say to Matt's spirit, "Matt, I'm leaving now. I want you to take over. Please watch over Cole and protect him." He would look at me, show me a thumbs-up, and give me a big wink. I would then leave the hospital feeling very peaceful.*

Sandy's nephew, Matt, who had been born severely handicapped and died at the age of twelve, was a great teacher of unconditional love for the whole family. Although there were no genetic ties between Matt and Cole, love has no boundaries, and there appears to have been a strong heart connection between these two boys. In the spirit world, our earthly distinctions of stepfamilies and in-laws are not recognized; there are only bonds of love and everyone is considered family. Sandy said, "I believe my love for Matt and my love for Cole was the connecting force."

Prayer Chains and Networks of Healers

Sandy set up a far-reaching network of healing by initiating a prayer chain that reached around the world. She called numerous family members and friends, asking them to pray for Cole and put him on their prayer list. These people called their family and friends, who kept the chain of love going by calling many others. We will never know the extent of these efforts—we can only imagine the growing network of strangers who took Cole into their hearts. Such unity of effort created a sense of oneness that affected Cole as well as everyone else involved.

Sandy also called numerous energy workers and asked them to send spiritual healing to Cole, requesting that they relay her message through their healing networks. So hundreds, perhaps thousands, of energy workers immediately began sending distant healing, which continued even past the twelve days of Cole's earthly life. They knew his spirit was still alive in heaven and able to receive their energy.

My Healing Session With Cole

On the fifth day, Grandma Sandy called asking me (Dr. Wesch) to come to Madison to do some healing sessions with Cole. My first impression of Cole seemed quite incongruent with the severity of his condition: he appeared fully developed, robust, and sturdy looking, though I knew he was fighting for his life. This beautiful baby lay inert on a small metal platform surrounded by medical equipment that extended from floor to ceiling. A jumbled maze of black electrical wires linked Cole to different monitors against the walls, and numerous tubes connected his little body to various machines of modern medicine. I found their constant blips and beeps intimidating and was quite overwhelmed by the whole scene.

It was difficult to even find a place to stand close to Cole. After some maneuvering, Sandy and I each found a place on opposite sides of Cole's little bed. We both put one hand on Cole's tiny chest and began sending healing energy into his heart.

Whenever I do spiritual healing, I close my eyes to tune out everything in the physical world so that I can focus my mind on perceiving the images of the interpenetrating spirit world. With my spiritual vision, I could see that Cole's room was filled with an intense spiritual light. It was really something to behold! It was so bright, it seemed like God was shining a spotlight on this scene. I felt awed to be in the presence of such divine love.

Of course, I wanted to understand how this could be, so I asked Spirit to show me the source of all this light. Glorious images came into my spiritual vision. The first was of Cole surrounded by concentric circles of angels that ascended higher and higher, extending further than I could see. The angels arranged themselves in tiers as if they were sitting in a stadium, and they sent a beautiful glow of divine love to Cole.

Then a second image flashed over the first. This time I saw thousands of light rays flowing into Cole's heart. Coming from every direction and angle, the rays were woven together to create a protective bubble of light around Cole. I asked, "What is this?" and heard, "This is the love energy created by all the positive thoughts, prayers, and healing work. Everything is as it should be."

A third image flashed in my mind. Mother Mary appeared in a glow of light. She was standing right next to me, her hand over mine on Cole's heart. At the same time, I heard the message, "I am the Mother of all Mothers. I held Cole to my heart at the moment of his birth. I am with him always. Be at peace."

I was immediately reminded of another message from Mother Mary. This one came to my friend Margaret Fry, a healer from England who does spiritual work with babies. Mother Mary said to Margaret, "I am present at the birth of every babe born on earth. I hold each one to my heart and kiss the infant's forehead." What joy to know Mother Mary was here for Cole!

Cole's aura extended far out from his body and was all aglow. His spirit energy formed a bright ball inside the large protective bubble of light. As I kept my hand on Cole's body, I received an image of a powerful magnet in the center of his heart. This magnet was drawing all the spiritual love to the very center of his being. He was definitely taking in all the love energy.

I felt both humbled and blessed to receive these glimpses of heaven right here on earth. It was amazing to see such scenes in this hospital setting; while chaos reigned at the human level, all was peaceful and beautiful at the spirit level. These very sacred moments with Cole eased the deep heartache I felt for Cole's family.

I returned the next day and could still perceive the tiers of angels, the light rays forming the bubble around Cole, and Mother Mary standing lovingly beside him. I had the understanding that all these spiritual beings, and many more than I could perceive, were there to watch over Cole's spirit during his time here on earth.

Sandy Receives a Healing

While in Madison, I encouraged Sandy to have her own Radiant Heart Healing session. She agreed, knowing that clearing some of her emotional pain would ultimately make her stronger, and she would then have the strength to continue helping Cole. Sandy's goal for the session was to release the tremendous fear she had about the possibility of Cole dying. She let go of not only the fear but also a great deal of grief and anger. Sandy described this mystical moment at the end of her healing session.

> *I was walking down this tunnel of light. It was so splendid! I could see Christ at the end of the tunnel. Everything was so vivid. I was enveloped with this loving energy. Everything was so peaceful, and I felt so safe. Never before or since have I felt so close to Christ. He looked young and had long hair. He didn't seem to have a body. There was just this incredible light!*

> *Christ gave me comfort and let me know that I'm loved. I don't know how long I was cradled in his energy of divine love. I just know I left the session feeling extremely peaceful. My fear was transformed.*

As we finished the session, I heard, "This is the peace that passes all understanding." I don't hear these words often, but when they come, I know Spirit, my client, and I have co-created a sacred moment of deep healing. Sandy allowed herself to go into that vulnerable place where fear is all-encompassing. In the eye of that storm, Christ appeared, and she received the gift of peace.

After releasing her fear, Sandy was able to return to the hospital and took this feeling of serenity with her. For the next seven days, Cole was in and out of crisis. Sandy remained very calm during this stressful time as she continued to do daily Radiant Heart Healing sessions with Cole. She believes the appearance of Christ helped her to be a pillar of strength, love, and encouragement to the rest of the family.

A Punch to the Shoulder

Ten days after Cole's birth, Grandma Sandy had a most unusual experience. She was home trying to get some rest after spending endless hours at the hospital. Early in the evening, she lay down on the family room couch and was praying for Cole.

> *I fell asleep on the couch and was suddenly awakened by a punch to the front of my shoulder. It really jarred me. In fact, it was so*

strong it woke me up. I looked around and nobody was in the room. I felt scared and very depressed. I didn't know what just happened, but I knew something was radically wrong.

The next day I went to see Cole at the hospital, and his energy felt so different to me. I could see that the light around him was very dim. His skin was yellow and flat and no brightness came from it. I felt he was no longer fighting for life. It seemed as if he was resigned to his death. I just knew his spirit was no longer there.

I always entrusted Cole's care to Matt, but now I could no longer see Matt at the foot of Cole's bed. I just couldn't get an image. It wasn't coming no matter how hard I tried. Matt was nowhere in that room. I couldn't understand why Matt was gone, and it really disturbed me.

Sandy walked out of the hospital that afternoon feeling like the weight of the world was on her shoulders. She was so down she could hardly put one foot in front of the other. Cole died during the night—approximately thirty-two hours after Sandy received the punch to her shoulder. Sandy believed it was just the machines that kept his little body alive during those hours. She said:

Months later, I realized that Cole's spirit left his body the night I felt that punch on my shoulder. Cole just wanted me to know he was leaving. I also realized why Matt's spirit was not in the room that last afternoon; I believe Matt left with Cole's spirit.

Cole Sends a Gentle Breeze

The night Cole died, Grandpa Dan and Grandma Sandy left the hospital in a state of deep grief and shock. They didn't know what to do or where to go to find comfort. Then, simultaneously, they both received the inspiration to drive to Olin Park, a place near the hospital that overlooks the capital building in Madison. This park holds a loving memory for them because years earlier Dan had proposed to Sandy at this very place.

They stood there holding each other and crying softly as they gazed mindlessly into the deep black of the night sky. It was very foggy and there was no wind. Sandy described the special moment that unfolded.

A light breeze went across my cheek. It was so gentle. I looked up at Dan and said, "That was Cole."

He answered, "Yes, I know. I felt it, too."

Dan and Sandy both started sobbing. It was a wondrous, breathtaking moment that will live in their hearts forever. They both believe this gentle breeze was Cole's way of telling them that he was not really gone.

A Test of Faith

Sandy was in total shock when Cole died. His death was so far from her expectations that she had great difficulty accepting the fact that he was no longer here on earth. She said:

> *I never thought Cole would die. For the whole twelve days, I believed he was going to have a complete and total recovery. My prayer was that he would come out of this a healthy baby boy, and I expected that to happen. After he died very early in the morning, I made lots of phone calls, telling my friends, "He's gone." I hardly cried the whole time I was doing this. In retrospect, I sounded like a robot.*

Sandy called another healer friend to tell her the news of Cole's passing. This woman picked up on Sandy's lack of emotion and said, "Sandy, I think you're really angry." Then Sandy started to sob and announced, "Damn it! This wasn't supposed to happen."

Sandy's faith was tested when her prayers for a complete recovery were not answered. She went through a period of feeling responsible and guilty for Cole's death. She questioned herself, saying, "What more should I have done? What did I do wrong? Why didn't the healing work?" It took months for her to let go of her expectations for a physical healing and accept that the healing did indeed work, but on the spiritual level. It just wasn't what she wanted or expected.

Sandy used Radiant Heart Healing as the core method for healing her grief about Cole, and she did numerous sessions of release work with another Radiant Heart Healer in Milwaukee. Sandy's goal was to energetically clear the pain, anger, guilt, and grief from her aching heart. Week after week, she kept making the choice to release the pain and fill up with love. Gradually, over the next year, she cleared the majority of her grief and accepted that Cole's journey unfolded exactly according to his soul plan. The messages she received from Cole through a spiritual medium helped her to achieve this acceptance.

Grandma Sandy's First Reading With a Spiritual Medium (Twelve Months After Cole's Death)

Medium: *Spirit says there is a male figure around you. This man is going through some very severe grieving, and he is very depressed. What is this man going through that he has so much depression? I can just feel it all around you.*

Sandy: *Our grandson, Cole, died and my husband, Dan, is just devastated.*

Medium: *There are a lot of spirits on the other side who are trying to lift him up. I'm seeing this big machine, and I'm hearing all this beeping. And I'm seeing death all around. I don't understand why I'm seeing all this. What is all this?*

Sandy: *Our grandson was hospitalized twelve days before he died. He was in the NICU, and the machines that you hear are the machines that kept him alive. [Crying]*

Medium: *Oh, honey. Cole is trying so hard to comfort you. Soooooo much.*

Sandy: *[Crying] I have a picture of him with me. This baby was very strong. He fought for twelve days to live. The whole time he was alive, he was so courageous.*

Medium: *Let me tell you something. Those twelve days that he was here—that was his mission. That was his purpose—to do what he had to do in those twelve days. And he celebrated his success. That was a success for him. And there is a sadness in that any of the family members felt so much pain. But everyone had this agreement prior to his being born that this would happen to give him this opportunity. Because what he did is going to save lives, or help others in the long run somewhere along the line. He was that brave and valiant.*

Sandy was very pleased that the medium saw a big machine and heard all this beeping. The fact that she could get these two specific details reassured Sandy and helped her believe that this woman was truly receiving information from Cole's spirit. The medium was also accurate when she said, "There's a male figure around you who is going through severe grieving and is very depressed." This information about Dan also helped Sandy trust that the medium was accurately tuning into her family situation.

Sandy was very comforted by this believable message from the spirit of her grandson. It gave her great joy to hear that Cole celebrated completing his mission during his twelve days here on earth, and that an agreement between Cole and the whole family gave him this opportunity. These two ideas brought her a sense of peace about Cole's death. She found it quite consoling to think that everything unfolded according to some spiritual plan. It was a plan she did not remember, but she felt something shift in her heart as she contemplated the idea of ancient promises being kept.

Of course, Sandy was uplifted to think that Cole's experience would help others and save lives sometime in the future. She wondered how this might play out. Needless to say, she had no answers to all her questions about this surprising notion. However, if this were true, then all the grief and heartache everyone went through would have some purpose. It was reassuring to think that something good could come out of something bad, and this thought brought Sandy peace of mind.

A Message While Golfing

Thirteen months after Cole's death, Grandma Sandy and Grandpa Dan were in Hilton Head, South Carolina, golfing with another couple. It was a crystal clear day with not a cloud in the sky. As they walked from one hole to the next, Sandy looked up and noticed a bank of clouds right over them. The sun was behind the clouds, and rays of the sun were streaming out. She shared this story with me.

I suddenly had the thought, "Oh, my God. That's Cole." I hadn't heard from him in a while, so I was sort of shocked at this thought. I'm a bit of a doubting Thomas, and I often doubt what I'm experiencing with spirits. So I said to Cole, "If this is really you, I want you to help Dan and me have the best drives we have ever had."

Moments later, Dan stepped up to the tee and did indeed hit his best drive ever. And he didn't even know I said this prayer to Cole. Then I stepped up to the tee and hit my best drive ever. I looked up at the clouds, did a high five to Cole, and said, "Thanks, Buddy."

Sandy laughed and continued her round of golf feeling very light-hearted. She didn't tell Dan or the other couple about this spirit communication from Cole. She just wanted to hold this little gift in her heart and treasure the feeling of love that flowed through her whole being.

Sandy's Second Reading With the Medium (Fifteen Months After Cole's Death)

Medium: *I recognize your face, so I know I've seen you before. However, you need to know that I never remember what I've told you. With each client, I bring through the information Spirit sends, and then I promptly forget everything. So with that said, let me tune into Spirit. I keep hearing this sound—beeow, beeow, beeow—these fetal monitors going off.*

Sandy: *That's Cole. He's my grandson, and that noise is the machines in the NICU.*

Medium: *They want you to know that your grandson's life was not in vain. He is a very valiant warrior on the other side—like a spirit—very strong and valiant. You should know that he is within the ranks of angels.*

Sandy: *Good.*

Medium: *Cole serves as a comforter on the other side. He comes to parents of children who are born with similar difficulties, and he is there. He is like a comforter. He not only comforts the parents, but he assists the little spirits to cross over. It's like this big, grand scheme. I don't know how to explain it to you, but this is very, very important.*

He's telling me that every time you say a prayer, he stands by your side. He listens to you. You must say lots of prayers because he says that he hears them.

Sandy: *Good.*

Medium: *When you say them, they spiral on the other side. It's like a kaleidoscope. It's just amazing what it does. It shifts the energies, which is very important.*

Sandy: *When Cole died, it was so hard on me, and I felt depleted of so much of my energy. A year ago at this time, I didn't realize completely yet that his death had meaning. And now that I know that, I've let go, and it isn't as hurtful as it was. So now, much of my energy has come back. I have a lot of energy.*

Medium: *Cole is showing me a video of you walking very fast. What do you do? Do you race walk or something?*

Sandy: *I walk very fast when I exercise.*

Medium: *Cole is saying he does the walks with you. Just so you are aware of that. So if you ever feel him around, you are right. He even wants to see you walk a bit more. He wants to see you stretch a bit more.*

Sandy: *That is very interesting. I was just thinking about that myself as I walked on the treadmill the other day.*

Medium: *He's telling me you should try Pilates. What's that?*

Sandy: *A stretching and strengthening exercise. That's cool! I just tried it last week.*

Medium: *He's talking about how your heart and his heart are the exact same thing. They are on the same wavelength. Some of those promptings you are receiving are coming from within yourself. It's like your higher self is connecting with him, and then you make the decision at the physical level.*

Sandy: *Cool.*

Sandy was fascinated to hear that Cole's spirit was helping the spirits of other dying babies, as well as comforting their parents. She had no idea the spirit of a baby could do such a thing, yet she believed this message. It was exciting for Sandy to think of Cole as a powerful spirit who had a purpose as he continued his soul journey on the other side. It was also very reassuring to think of Cole's death as part of a grand scheme, even if she couldn't yet grasp the big picture.

Sandy was also very pleased to hear that Cole's spirit knew she was saying a lot of prayers for him. After Cole's death, Sandy set aside time each day for saying prayers for his spirit, but she had no feedback about the effect of this ritual. It warmed her heart to know that the energy of her thoughts spiraled to the other side and assisted Cole's spirit in some way. This information strengthened her resolve to continue saying prayers daily.

Dan, Sandy, and Danita already believed that Cole's spirit routinely sent guidance to all the family members, but it was exciting for Sandy to hear that Cole sent her the inspiration to try a Pilates class. Intuitively, she already knew that Cole's spirit was right there with her as she walked on the treadmill, but she loved hearing the confirmation. This reading reinforced Sandy's trust that Cole was very much alive and still connected to the family.

Sandy's Third Reading With the Medium (Eighteen Months After Cole's Death)

After Cole's death, Sandy had many questions about the effectiveness of the Radiant Heart Healing sessions she did with Cole in the hospital. She decided to ask Cole's spirit about this matter during her next session with the same spiritual medium.

Sandy: *Did Radiant Heart Healing help Cole while he was here on earth?*

Medium: *Yes, absolutely. While you were doing the healing with him, a lot of that energy transferred. Have you seen how something affects something, and then little sparks go out and touch those that are around?*

Sandy: *Yes.*

Medium: *Cole is saying there were others around him who were also getting ready to cross over. They also received a spark of light from the healing energy you were sending to Cole. So this energy helped them also. They felt such joy about that. So the answer is emphatically YES! The Radiant Heart Healing did help Cole while he was here on earth. You need to continue to do it.*

Sandy: *Did Radiant Heart Healing help Cole with his transition?*

Medium: *Yes. The healing energy was like somebody literally holding his hand, so he could have an easier transition. It was like a boost of angels around him. So the answer is YES!*

Cole says, "The Radiant Heart Healing is one of the main methods that will help people to cross over. Your concentration was so strong when you were sending energy to me. The energy was like a beam of light. So how could you have failed? It could never have failed."

The Radiant Heart Healing helped him to transcend. It was very healing for him. Cole was of full knowledge of what he was supposed to be doing with himself. He tells me he needed to experience the power of love in that form.

This is so profound! People expected the healing to be in the physical. Radiant Heart Healing healed his spirit and his emotions. Cole's purpose has always been a mission of love.

Radiant Heart Healing

Sandy had great expectations about using Radiant Heart Healing with her grandson while he was in crisis. She believed with her whole heart and soul that doing the healing work would make a difference. Furthermore, she expected that difference to manifest at the physical level. This healing work did indeed make a difference, but the results of the healing impacted Cole at the spiritual level rather than the physical.

It took some time for Sandy to understand that the healing work was not in vain, even though Cole died. It was very reassuring to her to hear from Cole's spirit that the loving energy she sent him made it easier for him to make his transition. Sandy also loved hearing that the healing energy was like a boost of angels around him. These messages helped Sandy believe that her efforts did indeed make a difference for her grandson.

Spiritual healing works on many levels—spiritual, emotional, mental, and physical. The soul of the recipient has the power to decide the best use of the healing energy. Energy workers are trained to send healing energy and let go of any personal expectation as to how the recipient uses the energy. Spiritual healing may or may not achieve a cure at the physical level. Many times healing does not cure the physical problem, and the person does not get well. In these cases, it's a matter of faith to trust that healing is happening at other levels of being.

Cole made a fascinating statement: "I needed to experience the power of love in that form." Cole is telling us that it was part of his soul plan to experience all the love that was generated for him. This was an important part of his soul plan. What happened with all the Radiant Heart Healing sessions, the prayers, and distant healing was exactly right for him.

Sandy's Changes

Grandma Sandy talked about the many changes she made in her life after this experience of losing a grandchild. She spent a great deal of time in self-review, thinking about what's really important in life. One of the most important changes for Sandy is a new focus on love. She said:

> *I started using the mantra, "I am about love." I made a conscious choice to work fewer hours each week. I now choose to spend much more time with friends and family. Building loving relationships and being with all my loved ones have become much more important than spending so much of my time working. After losing Cole, I don't want to lose any more time with my other loved ones.*

This experience with Cole has greatly improved our marriage relationship. Dan chose to open his heart and start talking about his feelings, so we connected at a deeper level. I also opened my heart and let Dan see a more vulnerable part of me. We became so much closer after going through this experience with our grandson at the hospital. We really did a good job of supporting each other through our grief.

Because of her heart-opening experience with Cole, Sandy is less judgmental, more compassionate, and has become more open about expressing her thoughts and feelings to others. She has also become more generous of heart and devotes more time to philanthropic organizations— even raising money for a battered women's shelter. She discovered that money is not all that important, and it is certainly not the basis for happiness. Sandy also made significant changes in her prayer life.

Before Cole's birth, I used to pray only when I was in trouble and felt like I needed something from God. Now I pray every day and sometimes simply express my gratitude for all the blessings in my life. I also pray for many other people each day. I now have quite a long prayer list. Of course, Cole is always at the top of the list.

I sometimes worry that all of us might forget our experience with Cole and what we were supposed to take from it. I fear we might all go back to our old ways. I ask Cole to guide each of us so we stay on our new paths.

The Fabric of Our Family

Two years after Cole died, Sandy called me to tell me about the birth of his new baby brother, Carson. During this conversation, she reminisced about Cole and his impact on the family.

Cole's whole life and death represent what God is all about—love. Dan and I have absolutely no regrets about our process during the twelve days Cole was alive. It was love in its purest form. For the first time, I understood what unconditional love really means.

Cole's death was an agonizing experience to go through; however, our whole family has taken this event as an opportunity to grow emotionally and spiritually. Everyone is in much better shape because of what we've been through. When push comes to shove, the fabric of our family is woven much stronger than ever before.

Points to Ponder

This story portrays soul love as a powerful force that reaches across time and space to fortify the eternal family love bonds that exist between Cole's spirit and his parents, his grandparents, and his cousin Thomas. Cole uses inspiration, signs, messages, dreams, and even a spiritual medium to convey these important messages to his earthly family members:

- I still exist! There is no death!
- I am very much alive and surrounded by divine light.
- My entire being is filled with great joy, excitement, and love.
- Our connection is everlasting; we'll be together for eternity.
- Everything unfolded according to a divine plan.

From the other side, Cole inspires all his loved ones on earth to heal their grief and expand their consciousness; and so we see that, indeed, *love is stronger than death.*

Each soul comes to earth and begins life here in a tiny baby body. When a baby dies, loved ones usually see this new little being as a helpless infant and are unaware that he or she is really a magnificent, powerful soul who chose their family to accomplish some sacred purpose. In addition, most people are unacquainted with the idea that everyone who has a love connection with this baby made an ancient promise to support him or her in fulfilling a sacred purpose called the "divine plan." Our souls know the truth of these statements; however, at the human level, we have forgotten. Cole's story invites us to remember.

This story also gives us much to think about regarding the energy generated by prayers, positive thoughts, and the practice of distant healing. (In distant healing, the healer uses visualizations to send light and divine love from a remote location.) Thanks to Grandma Sandy organizing numerous prayer chains that then multiplied, thousands of people pray for Cole and send distant healing to this little baby from all over the world.

Positive thoughts, prayers, and all spiritual healing methods generate energy that vibrates at a very high frequency and is perceived by clairvoyants as either a very bright white light or, sometimes, colored rays. Both forms usually go unnoticed because their frequency is higher than the range seen by the human eye. However, because humanity is continually evolving to higher levels of consciousness, a growing number of people now have the ability to perceive this sacred light with their soul eyes.

If only Cole's family and the hospital staff could have seen the sacred light surrounding and protecting him those twelve days in the NICU. This little glimpse of heaven on earth would have brought them so much comfort. *Did you have an infant in the NICU for days, or even weeks or months? Perhaps you can also take comfort in the thought that all the prayers being said for your infant were surrounding him or her in divine light.*

After Cole's death, a spiritual medium informs Grandma Sandy that her spirit grandson stands by her side when she is praying and listens to every word. The medium even suggests that the energy of Sandy's prayers spirals to the other side and uplifts the energies around Cole, giving him a boost to accomplish his soul purpose there.

As you pray, can you imagine rays of white light radiating from your heart and flowing directly to your spirit baby? Can you trust that these rays of love energy can pierce the veil and connect with this powerful soul, who now exists somewhere out in the universe? Can you imagine the energy of your prayers giving this powerful soul assistance to complete a purpose on the other side? Trust that all of this is happening on a spiritual level that you cannot perceive with your human eyes. You don't have to know exactly how this works—you only have to say a prayer.

Your baby is now a light being—a powerful soul who can come and go at will across the veil. I invite you to pray for this magnificent being who, like Cole, has the ability to come close, listen to every word, and then once again flow out into the universe. If you are at a loss about how to pray for your spirit baby, I recommend this simple prayer:

To the spirit of my dear, sweet baby in heaven,

I love you, and our heart connection is eternal. I lovingly release you to your eternal journey in the spirit world. I trust that my forever love will continue to support you until we meet again somewhere in time.

Cole's story also clearly demonstrates that spiritual healing is not about the survival of the physical body; rather, it's about the completion of the soul's purpose—while in physical form and as a spirit on the other side. In this story, Grandma Sandy sends healing energy to her precious grandson while praying for him to live. She expects the healing sessions and all the prayer energy to make a difference at the physical level. When Cole dies, Sandy has a crisis of faith.

Together, Cole and a spiritual medium explain to Grandma Sandy that the prayer chains and energy sessions healed Cole's spirit and his emotions. They also tell her that he accomplished his soul purpose by experiencing the power of love from all these sources: prayers, distant healing, Mother Mary, a host of angels, Sandy's deceased nephew, and his human family, who spent twelve days at his bedside in the hospital.

Did you pray for your baby to live, only to have your precious infant die anyway? Perhaps, like Sandy, you also had a crisis of faith. I invite you to trust that healing did occur—spiritually, mentally, and emotionally—even if there was no evidence of improvement on the physical level.

After the death of an infant, loved ones often ask, "Why did this happen? What's the meaning of the tragedy?" Understanding the concept of a pre-birth soul plan helps grieving loved ones find answers to these questions. The soul plan defines the spiritual purpose for the baby, as well as for all the loved ones involved in the experience of infant death. Of course, we have to look at the situation with soul eyes to discover the spiritual purpose—looking with human eyes will guarantee that you will miss the answer you seek.

Cole's spiritual purpose is many-faceted: he came to 1) be a magnet for love in all its forms, 2) teach others about unconditional love, 3) help other dying babies and children transition to the other side, and 4) bring comfort to their devastated parents. Like the Inca spirit babies, Cole is a powerful healer. While this is true, each of Cole's family members still has lessons to learn and soul growth to accomplish as they move forward on their individual healing journeys after his death. The ripple effect is expansive.

I invite you to expand your thinking about the death of your beloved infant. *Imagine that you and your baby had a pre-birth agreement to go through this experience of infant death together. Can you embrace the idea that everything unfolded according to a divine plan? What spiritual lessons are you learning as you seek to heal your grief? What shifts in consciousness (soul growth) are needed so you can be at peace about your loss? Without a doubt, the death of your baby has meaning and purpose. Let yourself ponder what that might be.*

CHAPTER TWO

A Woman With a Mission

You have to get beyond the pain.
It's not that you will ever get over your child,
but you will get over the pain.
—Sue, Jake's Mother

The true measure of a life is about how many people you touch and the love that is generated. Does this statement apply to a baby who lived only a very short time? Indeed, it does—especially if you view the situation through soul eyes. As you will see in this next story, Jake, a baby who lived only twenty-one hours and thirty-three minutes, touched many people and generated much love while he was alive.

More importantly, as a spirit baby, Jake is continuing to touch people, open hearts, and inspire love. Like the Inca spirit babies, Jake is a powerful healer for his mother, Sue, who has a mission to first heal her own grief and then help others to heal grief after the loss of an infant. For the past ten years, Sue has been sharing the many miracles of her healing journey so others can learn from her experience. Each time she tells Jake's story, it's like dropping another pebble in the pool—the healing ripples are far-reaching.

Premonitions Disregarded

This young mother had an inner knowing about her baby's death. Sue has always had a sixth sense, and often she just "knows stuff" without having any real evidence. For example, she sometimes gets a sick feeling in her stomach and has a premonition that something is very wrong; then she will get a phone call that somebody in the family has died. In our initial interview, Sue talked about the warning signals she received about Jake.

I knew the whole last month that something was going to be wrong with Jacob's birth. I knew, but I denied it because it was too painful to contemplate such a thought. Looking back, I can see the warning signs that I ignored at the time.

The first forewarning was a weird experience that happened at work three weeks before my due date. And in the bathroom of all places! I had this daydream, but it was very vivid and seemed so real. I got the feeling that something was seriously wrong with the baby, and I would have to call 911. As I envisioned myself dialing the emergency number, I just knew my baby would die. When this dire thought came into my mind, I started sobbing. Of course, I pulled myself back together, returned to my desk, and dismissed the whole thing.

The second warning occurred in a conversation with my sister the night before Jacob was born. I found myself asking her, "Why do stillbirths happen?" Looking back, it seems very eerie that I was asking such a question. Medically, Jacob is considered stillborn because he lived less than twenty-four hours.

21 Hours and 33 Minutes of Love

The birth and death of their first-born child has been a life-changing event for both Sue and her husband, Steve. The pregnancy was perfectly normal until the week before Sue's due date. Then she noticed the baby was much less active and insisted on some testing to see if everything was okay. The doctors determined that the baby was indeed in distress and did an immediate C-section delivery. They told Sue and Steve that a section of the placenta had died and caused a severe lack of nutrition for the baby. It is a very rare medical phenomenon with no hope of recovery for the baby if the condition has progressed too far. The doctors did not expect Jacob to survive at all but he lived twenty-one hours and thirty-three minutes.

During this precious time Jake, Sue, and Steve were surrounded in love and supported by family. Sue described this time.

Steve and I are both from very large Catholic families—we are each one of seven kids. Many of them live right here in town, so most of the family came to the hospital to support us. The love I felt from everybody was just incredible—it surrounded us during those twenty-one hours. Even the nurses kept commenting about all the love.

I have no memory of the two hours immediately after they told me Jake wasn't going to make it. My sisters tell me I let out the most horrible cry they ever heard. It was more like a wail, and it pierced the hearts of every family member present. Steve and I held each other as we cradled Jake and just cried and cried.

Then at one point, I stopped crying and started being a proud mom. Looking back, I still don't know where I got the wisdom and the strength to do what I had to do. It just came from some place deep inside of me.

The priest on call at the hospital was a family member, so we held a baptismal ceremony right there in the neonatal unit. Everyone present in the family was able to hold Jake, even if it was for just two seconds. He was surrounded by the love everyone showered on him.

Jacob lived through the first night with life support machines keeping him alive. The doctors were very clear there was no hope of him improving. Sue and Steve were united in their decision to take their son off life support. They made this painful decision with courage and strength, knowing this was best for their son. Released from all the equipment, Jacob lived one hour more. Sue and Steve were alone with Jacob during his last hour; they held him and talked to him the entire time. Sue described these cherished moments.

That hour is the most precious memory we have of being with our son. It was a time of sharing our love with him. We had the privilege of being able to hold him and love him even though we knew he was dying.

We held him and talked to him as if he could understand. We told him, "It's okay to go. Great-Grandpa Jack will be there with you. Great-Aunt Flossie will be with you, too. Go find daddy's friend Doug, who just crossed over. He will take you fishing." Steve is an avid fisherman and often fished with Doug. Steve had a dream of teaching our son to fish, so he talked to Jacob about fishing in the spirit world.

Both Sue and Steve opened their hearts and shared with Jake all of the hopes and dreams they had developed during the nine months of pregnancy. Jacob listened with his eyes wide open.

Jake couldn't speak with words, but his eyes spoke volumes. Actually, he had his eyes wide open the majority of the time that he stayed here with us. It was so unusual because most newborn babies keep their eyes closed. As I looked into his eyes, I remember thinking I was looking right into his soul. I truly felt our soul connection.

When Jake was first delivered, there was a moment when he was clinically dead. The doctors revived him—pulled him back, so to

*speak. I believe he saw heaven in that moment and then came back
to tell us through his eyes.*

Sue and Steve were mesmerized as they looked into Jacob's eyes. Their
eyes, as well as their words, communicated their deep love for him. Their
soul link with Jacob is very strong because of the intensity and depth of
the bond created during this time when soul love flowed back and forth
between their hearts.

Precious Moments Recorded

Sue and Steve have a video recording of some of their most precious
moments with Jake. This video is one of Sue's treasures, and she feels a
deep connection with Jake's spirit each time she watches it. Of course, she
has watched it hundreds of times during her healing journey. She also loves
to share it with anyone who will take the time. Sue commented about the
video, "It's eight minutes of 'I love you' in eight millimeter." Sue described
the video.

*I have complete memory loss of the several hours right after they told
me Jake wouldn't make it. I know this is my mind's way of protecting
me from the most horrendous pain I've ever experienced. So the
video has become extremely important to me, because it has filled in
some of the memory gaps.*

*For instance, I was afraid I didn't tell Jake I loved him while he was
alive. Then I watched the video and there I am saying, "Mama loves
you, Jake." In fact, I said it over and over again, and it's all on film
so I won't forget.*

*There's a scene on the video where Steve and I are talking to Jake,
and he has his eyes closed. I ask Jake, "Can you open your eyes?"
And he did! This scene is so special to us. The doctors deemed this a
miracle because they had just examined Jake and found that he was
in massive organ failure. There was no brain function at all, yet he
turned his little head when I talked to him, and he opened his eyes
when I asked him. And we have it all on video!*

*Jake has his eyes open about half the time on our eight-minute video.
He looks very alert and rather all-knowing. He keeps looking at us
as if he's listening and taking in everything we're saying to him. I
also have the feeling his soul was speaking to us through his eyes. He
was saying, "I'm going to be okay." His eyes were just so incredible!
I love watching the video just so I can see his eyes again.*

Healing Grief

Sue has been incredibly passionate and creative about finding ways to heal her heart-wrenching grief. Talking about Jake has been a very big part of her healing journey. These are her words just nineteen months after Jacob's death:

> *You know, people don't get it about grief. They just don't get it! In the beginning, I had this deep need to talk about Jake and talk about my grief. Most people didn't know how to respond to me. They seemed to think I was a little crazy. I wanted to talk about him, and I wanted to do things for him. I wanted to celebrate his birth and his existence. You know, Lincoln is dead and Washington is dead. We honor their lives by celebrating them on President's Day. So why shouldn't I honor Jake? We celebrated his first birthday with a big family party, and it was a very healing event.*
>
> *I have this deep fear that people might forget about Jake, so I have insisted that my family talk about him—both his birth and his death. When we talk about him, it honors me as his mother. I just tell everyone this is what I need. I also tell them that he is here in spirit, so pay attention because he is sending messages all the time. I even tell everyone the messages I get from Jacob's spirit.*
>
> *In the beginning, Steve and I were sad all the time. I wanted my friends and relatives to understand that talking about Jake didn't make us sad. Actually, talking about Jake is what helped us to heal.*

Cosmic Love Notes From Jacob

Messages started coming from Jacob's spirit almost immediately after his death. These messages were also a very important part of Sue's healing journey. At the funeral, another family member received a vision of Sue's Aunt Flossie holding Jake and showing him around heaven. It brought Sue great comfort to imagine Jacob being held and loved by her favorite aunt, who was now on the other side.

The first Christmas after Jake's death, Sue's family gave her a very precious gift—an artist's drawing of Aunt Flossie holding Jacob in her arms. Joy and love flowed into Sue's aching heart as she gazed at this portrait in amazement. The family explained an artist had created it as he looked at individual photographs of Aunt Flossie and Jacob. Sue has this portrait hanging on her bedroom wall, where she can see it first thing in the morning when she wakes up and last thing at night as she goes to sleep.

Whenever she looks at this portrait of the two of them together, she gets a feeling that Aunt Flossie is saying, "I've got him, and he's just fine."

The first weeks after the funeral, Sue lay in bed crying for hours at a time. One afternoon she heard a child's voice say, "Mommy, don't cry. I don't like you crying." At first, she thought she was just making it up or, worse yet, going crazy. She looked around to see if there was anyone in the room. No one was there. Sue intuitively knew the child's voice was Jacob's spirit and that he was communicating with her. During our interview, Sue appeared quite nonchalant as she said, "I talk to Jacob and Jacob talks to me."

Sue goes about her daily life fulfilling her responsibilities as a wife, a homemaker, and the manager of a large department at a bank. Then, in the quiet times, she has these conversations with Jake. I found this quite remarkable given that Sue has no training in meditation practices, psychic development, or spirit communication. She's a very down-to-earth career woman who seems to think it's quite normal to have these ongoing conversations with the spirit of her son. Sue is often in awe of the messages she receives. She noted, "Jake seems to have wisdom beyond what a newborn baby could have. His messages often contain such phenomenal insights. They sometimes seem like something a very wise sage would say."

Sometimes Sue hears just a short message from Jacob, and at other times, she participates in a longer dialogue, like this one:

Jacob: *Mommy, don't cry.*

Sue: *Jacob, I miss you so much. I wanted to teach you everything.*

Jacob: *But you did, Mommy. You taught me love.*

Sue: *Jacob, I don't know if this is me talking or if this is really you. You sound just like me.*

Jacob: *Of course, Mom. Who else would I sound like?*

Sue laughed with genuine joy and delight as she reported this conversation with her son. It obviously gave her much pleasure to have Jacob being profound and humorous at the same time. His words were such a surprise! She knew she did not make it up in her own mind. Sue also explained the deeper meaning she derived from Jake's message.

Love is everything. If you know love, you have learned everything. What else is there to know? When you are on your deathbed all you need is love.

A Musical Message

Sue flows easily with her emotions—she cries when her heart is touched, sparkles with excitement, and breaks into spontaneous laughter in humorous moments. Sue's joyous laughter bubbled up as she related this favorite anecdote about a musical message that warmed and cheered her heart.

Several months after Jacob's death, Sue remembered how she would sit in the baby's room rocking in the rocker and talking to Jacob while he was in the womb. Often she would read a Dr. Seuss book to him. This book was especially written for mothers to read aloud to a baby in utero.

One day, Sue felt inspired to go into Jacob's room, rock in the rocker, and read the Dr. Seuss book aloud to her spirit baby. She was halfway through the book when his musical baby gym just spontaneously started playing. She knew she had not turned it on or wound it up. Right away, she understood this was another message from Jacob. She sat holding the book to her heart, crying tears of joy. Sue answered Jacob's message saying, "Thanks for letting me know you're here. I guess you still like this little book. Well, I still enjoy reading it to you."

The Jake of My Dreams

Just three months after Jacob's death, Sue received some strong guidance from Jacob while she was shopping. She wanted to buy an angel picture or angel statue that would represent Jake. However, all she could find were girl angels. One day Sue went shopping at a craft fair. She was walking past a booth of framed artwork when something told her to stop. She went in, and way in the back, she found a picture of a little boy angel with short blonde hair who looked to be about three or four years old. The little boy angel looked exactly the way Jake appeared in her dreams! It was just amazing! She sent a message to her son saying, "Thanks, Jake. You helped me find your angel picture. I can't believe it! I'm so happy you did this for me!"

Sue told her story about Jake to the cashier, who was very touched. She brought out a catalog of Nancy Noel's artwork and found the picture Sue had just purchased. The name of the picture was "Jacob!" Sue was amazed at the coincidence and felt an intense curiosity about the artist who captured her "dream Jacob" so perfectly. She looked on the Internet to find out more about the artist Nancy Noel and discovered a book with the same boy angel named Jacob on the front cover. Sue searched numerous area bookstores and finally found a copy. The book, entitled *All God's*

Creatures Go To Heaven, is the story of a little boy named Jacob who dies and goes to heaven, where he becomes an angel and takes care of all the little spirit animals that live there.

The book, filled with beautiful pictures of children as angels, offers great consolation and hope to grieving parents and has become Sue's favorite book for healing her grief. She felt inspired to give a copy to each member of her family for Christmas and signed each book, "Love, Jacob."

Finding Pennies—A Sign From Jake

Early in her healing journey, Sue went to a one-day seminar about overcoming grief. She brought home these messages: "Coincidences don't just occur; they are actually little messages or signs guided by Spirit." "Everything happens for a reason." And, "Pay attention to everything that happens around you."

This information strengthened what Sue already believed about signs and messages from our loved ones on the other side. She began to pay more attention to the moment rather than to her thoughts of grief. She knew she had to be alert and focused on the here-and-now as she went about her daily life so she would not miss any signs from Jacob.

The first thing she noticed was that she began to find pennies. She found the first one on the sidewalk as she walked to work. Then she found another one on the floor of a restaurant. Then she found another, and another, and another. Soon she was finding pennies everywhere! This had never happened to her before Jake's passing. Sue trusted that these pennies were a sign from Jacob saying, "Hello, I'm still here." These were welcome messages, and each time she would smile and mentally say, "Hello, I love you, Jake!" She was thankful for each penny; these uplifting signs helped ease her heartache.

One day, a significant scenario unfolded. Sue told it like this:

> *This one day I was really missing Jake, and I desperately wanted a penny from him. I kept looking diligently, but nothing appeared. I was attending a baby shower for a friend, and I was walking through the atrium area of a bank lobby. With each step, I kept my eye out for another penny. Nothing. I walked through the atrium, up a flight of stairs, and stood on the balcony overlooking the path I had just traveled. I stood there telling another friend how much I was missing Jake and wishing he would throw me a penny. At that very moment, we both spotted a shiny penny right below us! It was*

right on the path I just walked! It was not there when I first came through, and no one else had come by that way. I ran down the steps with such joy to pick up that penny. I knew in my heart it had to come from Jake!

I'm always so grateful when I find another penny. It strengthens my belief that Jake is still very much alive and sending me love whenever and wherever he can.

Sue's Healing Dreams

Immediately after the funeral, Sue began to have many healing dreams about Jacob. During his visitations, they would take long walks together, and he always put his left hand in her right hand. When she looked at the pictures from the NICU, she saw that even then she always held his left hand in her right hand.

Sue soon realized that she would only dream about Jacob when she needed something. Early in her grief process, she felt a great loss because she never got to breastfeed Jacob. Sue knew it was a desire that she could never fulfill; yet she kept obsessing about it. She couldn't let go of it. Then, she had a dream about breastfeeding her son. She got to experience what it was like to hold him in her arms and nurse him. She awoke with a vivid memory of every feeling and every wonderful moment in the dream. At the end of the dream, Jake said to her, "Is that okay now? I only did it because you needed it. I didn't need it." She woke up laughing at her son's message. It was such a healing dream! Breastfeeding Jacob was no longer an issue.

Months later, Sue was grieving because she would never get to see Jake grow up. When she tried to go to sleep at night, she would be thinking about all the different stages in his life that she would never get to see. She would never see him take his first steps, or learn to ride a bike, or go to kindergarten. She would never see him grow up and get married or have children of his own.

Then one night, Sue had a dream that she was hugging an older man who looked about sixty-five years old. She knew it was Jake. She also saw herself at the age of one hundred and two. As mother and son continued to embrace, they gazed into each other's eyes and exchanged their great soul love. Then, right before her eyes, Jake got younger and younger until he was a baby in her arms. This dream gave her the gift of seeing him at all the stages of his life. What a miracle! Even though it was a dream, this experience eased her aching desire to see him grow up in the physical. Sue also told me:

> *Since this dream, I feel like I'll live a long time. I always used to think I would die young, and I was very afraid of dying. Now it doesn't matter when I die or if I die. My fear of death just vanished. I believe that dream was a healing message from Spirit, and it was just what I needed. I'm watching how I always get whatever I need for my healing.*

Jacob's Memory Book

During our interview, Sue proudly showed me Jake's memory book that she created as part of her healing journey. It was obvious that Sue put her heart and soul into creating this treasure of pictures and stories recording Jake's short time here on earth. Sue believes the process of constructing this book was one of the most healing things she did for herself. Her face glowed, and there was a special light in her eyes as she talked about making the album.

> *I was afraid people would forget Jacob or deny that he ever existed. The very idea made my heartache even worse. I wanted something to show people about my son. I knew I needed something physical—something we could all see and touch and hold. One day, as I looked at the collection of his baby pictures, I felt inspired to put them in a baby memory book. Once I started, I just followed my heart and did what felt right to me.*

> *I say I followed my heart, but I really think Jake's spirit inspired me to make the album, and he was there as I did each page. With Jake's guidance, it was so easy. I know he showed me how to do the page layouts. The clerks at the scrapbook store saw the book and said, "This is incredibly well done. It's better than what some of our teachers can do."*

> *In the beginning, I expected the album would be limited; after all, we didn't have very many pictures since Jake lived only twenty-one hours. Months later, I felt guided to include some of my significant healing experiences in the book. So I took pictures or made special art projects to help me remember those meaningful moments.*

> *My favorite page is filled with pictures of me lying in the snow making snow angels. The first white blanket of winter covered the ground, and every tree branch was laden with inches of white fluff.*

It looked like a fairyland when a friend and I went to visit Jake's grave in the early morning. I had always wanted to make a snow angel for Jake, much like I had remembered doing so many times as a child. So I did! My friend joined me and took pictures. Such fun! We laughed and talked to Jake's spirit the whole time. "Look at what Mommy is doing. We're making angels for you, Jake. Do you like this one with the big wings?"

I just loved creating this book, and I love looking through it. It does my heart good to know I will never forget. And like any other mom, I'm so proud to show people my Jacob book.

A Reading With a Spiritual Medium

Sue's session with a medium was truly a date with destiny. Sue described herself as a big-time skeptic regarding spiritual mediums, but she decided to go just for fun. This was her first session of this kind, and she didn't believe anyone could contact Jake. She decided to keep very quiet and not tell the medium anything so as not to give her any clues. Coincidently, the session was scheduled just three days before Jacob's first birthday. Here are the important messages from the session.

Medium: *They are showing me lots of white tulips—white tulips everywhere. What's with the white tulips?*

Sue: *I don't know.*

Medium: *There's a little boy here. He looks to be about three years old with blonde hair. Have you been going to the cemetery a lot? I see you walking there. As you walk in, he walks along with you, and he holds your hand. He puts his left hand in your right hand. He just loves to hold your hand!*

Sue: *Yes, I go to the cemetery to visit the grave of my son, Jacob. He only lived twenty-one hours.*

Medium: *He's all excited about some celebration. He keeps showing me balloons and talking about this celebration. He says he plans to be there. I can't tell what he's talking about.*

Sue: *I know what he's talking about. We are having his first birthday celebration in three days. We have planned a big family party, and it's going to be a very happy time. Lots of family will be attending, and I'm planning to have lots of balloons.*

Medium: *He's very happy about this! What are those things that spin? They stand on a stick and the wind blows them. He is showing me these things, but I can't think of the name of them.*

Sue: *It must be pinwheels.*

Medium: *Oh, yes. Thanks. He's showing me pinwheels. He just loves those pinwheels! What's with the pinwheels?*

Sue: *I put pinwheels on his grave last month for the July 4th celebration.*

Medium: *Well, he really likes them. He says, "Thanks, Mom. I love to watch them whirl."*

Sue: *I'll go out and buy one for his birthday.*

Medium: *He doesn't want just one. He wants three of them! He's very emphatic about this.*

Sue: *[Laughing] Okay, Jake, I'll buy three pinwheels! I have a question. Are there any animals with Jake?*

Medium: *Yes, there's a little brown dog with him. Jake tells me the dog's name is Butch.*

Sue: *[Crying] Oh, My God! I can't believe it! I had a dog named Butch when I was a child. I'm an animal lover, and I've had lots of animals all my life. Butch was my very favorite of all time. We had a really close connection. After he died, he used to come visit me in my dreams for years. He'd be running and playing, just like when he was here.*

Medium: *He's a little dog, but he has a ferocious spirit. He's sitting on his hind legs and making a funny motion with his front paws. What's he doing?*

Sue: *[Crying] We taught him to sit up and do patty-cake. It was his favorite trick. This really has to be Butch. [Laughing] Wow, I'm so happy that Butch is with Jake!*

Medium: *Yes, they are having many happy times together over there. They really love each other!*

Sue was blown away with her reading. The medium described Jake as Sue always saw him—a little boy about three or four years old with blonde hair. There were so many important details in this reading that made the messages believable to Sue: Jake holding her hand as she went walking in the cemetery, the medium pulling the name Butch out of thin air, Butch doing his patty-cake trick, and Jake describing the pinwheels at the gravesite. Sue was also thrilled to hear that Jacob was looking forward to his birthday celebration. This confirmed for her that Jake was indeed around and able to know that she was planning the party.

The information that came through about Butch was both astounding to Sue and very comforting. She hadn't seen Butch and Jake together in any of her dreams. However, she believed the messages that came through the medium and was so delighted to know that Butch and Jake were playing together in the spirit world. Sue explained.

> *I believe my love for Butch and my love for Jake was the connecting force for the two of them to find each other in heaven. Butch died when I was in my teens, and he still comes to visit me a couple times a year in my dreams. I've had lots of animals over the years, but Butch is the only one who keeps coming back in my dreams. We had such a strong connection.*

The white tulips mentioned at the beginning of the reading were a bit of a mystery for Sue. For days after the reading, Sue kept questioning her relatives, trying to see if there was anyone on the other side who loved white tulips; she thought maybe it was a clue about some deceased relative who was with Jake. No one could make a connection. A few weeks later, it dawned on Sue that she and Steve had planted a special tree in honor of Jake and planted white tulips all around it. The flowers were long gone with the summer's heat, but would bloom again next spring. Jake was acknowledging his special memorial by showing the medium the white tulips. Sue completely missed the clue given by her spirit son; this is called psychic amnesia and happens frequently during readings.

Jacob's First Birthday Party

Sue listened to her own heart when she decided to give a party for Jacob's first birthday. She knew others might think it was rather a bizarre idea, but she was determined to overcome their discomfort and involve them in a celebration of her son's birth. She invited only close relatives and explained to all of them that she intended this to be a party to honor the memory of Jacob.

Everyone turned out, and the traditional ice cream and birthday cake were served. Some people brought money gifts, which Steve and Sue donated to the Infant Loss Program at the hospital where Jacob was born. Sue managed to carry off the party with great dignity, and it was a very healing event for the whole family. However, she whispered candidly to me, "We lit the candles and blew them out, but I just couldn't bring myself to sing happy birthday. So we left that part out."

Before the party, Sue and Steve bought helium balloons and took them to the cemetery. They put a note in one of the balloons that said, "Happy Birthday, Jacob. Love from Mom and Dad." As they let the balloons go, they both had a knowing that Jacob would get the message. And with a laugh, Sue put three pinwheels in a prominent place in their backyard.

Sue's three-year-old niece Xena brought another supply of helium balloons so the whole family could symbolically send their love to Jacob in heaven. Before letting the balloons go, Xena insisted that Sue make a puppy dog balloon to send to her cousin in heaven. Someone captured a great picture of everyone waving to Jacob's spirit as the little puppy dog and the rest of the balloons went flying high into the cloudless blue sky. Sue laughed joyfully as she showed me the picture in Jacob's memory book.

Sue's mother even got into the spirit of the party. First, she had everyone blowing bubbles; then she invited Sue's sister-in-law to try to catch them. Of course, it was an impossible assignment. Each time she tried, the bubbles burst and left a sticky substance all over her fingers. Sue's mother then announced with great wisdom: "Trying to catch the bubbles is like trying to touch Jacob. It's an impossible assignment. As soon as you touch the bubble, it bursts. Then you can't see it but you can feel it. That's just like Jacob's spirit. You can't see him but you can feel him."

Sue went to sleep that night feeling a warm glow in her heart. She had taken a big risk inviting everyone to this event. At the end of the day, she knew the risk was worth every bit of the stress and worry she went through while planning the party. Sue said:

> *A big reason people came was that I talked about it so much. It was important to me, and I told my family how much I wanted it. They decided to come because they cared about me. It was worth it because each member of the family experienced a big healing that afternoon, exactly the outcome I wanted.*

> *Now I can remember Jacob's special day with joy instead of grief. My joy comes from recalling all the wonderful scenes we created that day as we shared tears, laughter, love, and healing. And I know in my heart that Jacob was also sharing all the same feelings. What a great day!*

A Letter From Dr. Kate

Sue had another creative idea as she concluded the first year of her healing journey. She asked everyone involved with Jacob to write letters describing their experience with his birth and death. She told each person, "You might think this will make us sad, but it's what will help us heal." She even asked Jacob's doctors, nurses, social workers, and the priest. Many people responded, and Jacob's memory book now has a whole collection of these heart-warming letters. They really showed Sue and Steve that Jacob touched many lives in a very deep way.

About this same time, Sue stopped by the hospital and paid a visit to Dr. Kate, the special-care baby doctor who attended Jake in the NICU. She was also the person who had the difficult task of informing Steve and Sue that Jake was not going to make it. Dr. Kate said to Sue, "I know you have no idea how much Jacob has touched my life. I have never before been touched by a baby like this. Jacob came to me in a dream just three days after he died. I'm pressed for time right now but I will tell you all about the dream in my letter. I'm so honored that you asked me to contribute something for Jacob's book."

Then Sue said, "With all the babies that come through this hospital I'm amazed that you bonded with him."

Dr. Kate responded, "I didn't bond with him; he bonded with me!"

Sue was quite stunned as she finished this conversation with Dr. Kate. She could hardly believe that Jake's spirit visited Dr. Kate in a dream. Her logical mind had lots of questions: *How could this be? How did Jake connect with Dr. Kate? What was the meaning of this visitation to the doctor?* She had all these questions, but she had no answers. It was indeed another mystery. Of course, by this time she was getting used to all the mystery surrounding Jake.

Dr. Kate attended Jake's one-year memorial service held at the hospital. At the end of the ceremony, she gave Sue the letter for Jacob's memory book. Dr. Kate's message was printed on beautiful paper with hearts at each corner and a colorful child's train chugging across the bottom of the page. Just the stationery was something to behold.

Dear Jake:

A very long time ago, when I was a little girl living in Montana, our local humane society visited my primary school. They brought bunnies and puppies and birds and a snake and taught us all about pets. Near the end of the day, Sister Kathryn showed us a video that suggested what happened to animals that did not find a home. I was outraged.

I decided I needed to take this up with God. I said a prayer out loud asking God to take the very next puppy to heaven and save him for the most special kid ever. My dad said he was sure God would choose a beagle. I was sure He would name him Pete.

It would be a very long time before I remembered that day. It was a few nights after you died. I was sleeping at the hospital on night duty when I had a vivid dream. I was watching a tiny boy with green eyes and a naked bum sharing ice cream with a little hound dog. There was lots of howling and giggling, rolling and licking.

It was you and Pete. I remembered my prayer.

My last foggy glance was of you and Pete curled up together fast asleep in a sunny meadow under a palm tree with white feather leaves.

Thank you, Jake, for being that puppy's someone very special.

Thank you for my dream.

And thank God for giving you Pete and white feather wings.

He has very important plans for you indeed.

Your Doctor Kate

Sue read this letter with tears of joy steaming down her face and love filling her heart. Then she sat in stunned silence for a very long time trying to assimilate Dr. Kate's awesome message. Sue read the last line of the letter again and again, "He (God) has very important plans for you indeed." This was not a new idea to her, and she took time to contemplate it again. *Was there really a plan? What was Jacob's part in the plan? As Jacob's mother, what was her part in the plan? Was she doing all she needed to do to help the plan unfold?* Again, Sue had more questions than she had answers. Even though she was mystified, it was very comforting to think that Jake's death was part of a bigger plan.

Healing With the Next Baby

Sue and Steve both wanted children, so they decided to have another baby as soon as possible after the tragedy with Jake. Sue said:

We could not get pregnant fast enough. We always wanted children, so of course, losing our first-born was a terrible blow. Naturally, we worried about not being able to get pregnant again. We felt so blessed to conceive rather quickly. Chad was born just thirteen months after Jacob. I was so thrilled because my biological clock was ticking—I was thirty-seven when Jake was born and thirty-eight when Chad was born.

Sue used the same obstetrician and hospital that she had when Jake was born. When her C-section was scheduled, a most unusual thing happened. The word spread and soon all the same doctors and nurses who were present for Jake's delivery signed up to participate in Chad's delivery. The female surgeon doing the C-section even came in on her day off to be part of the team. Sue explained:

Chad's delivery was a great healing for the whole team of medical professionals. They were all hurting from their experience with Jake, and being part of a successful birth was very helpful for healing their grief.

All the members of my family who came to the hospital for Jake also came to celebrate Chad's birth. It was very healing for them too. We had quite a roomful of people!

Losing a child made me enjoy being pregnant even more. I noticed every movement with Chad and did not complain about any of the discomforts of pregnancy. This time Steve and I both knew the reality of death, and we understood that we might or might not get to hold this baby. This made us appreciate every little thing about the pregnancy.

We also appreciate every little thing about Chad since his birth. We certainly do not take him for granted. His crying doesn't bother us. We even enjoy it because we didn't get to hear Jake cry. We don't mind getting up for his middle-of-the-night feedings. In fact, we just enjoy every waking minute spent with Chad.

I believe that more of my unresolved grief was cleansed by Chad's birth. Of course, I made great strides on my healing journey long before he was born. Since Chad's birth, I don't feel Jake around so much. I guess that's because I don't need him like I did before.

A Father's Healing Journey

Jacob's father, Steve, is a very sensitive man with artistic talent. Right after high school, he was accepted into an art program where he was one of the few chosen. He had to turn down the opportunity because he couldn't afford to go to college. He works long hours in construction to provide for his family, and he often yearns for free time to use his creative abilities. Steve talked about his grief.

I had no idea the loss of a baby could be as devastating as it was. In the beginning, it felt good to be working just to keep my mind busy. However, I felt physically drained for months afterwards—just sort of sluggish. I didn't seem to have as much ambition as before. It's not that I was lazy, but I felt like I needed a nap at eleven a.m. every day. I just felt burned out all the time. I guess I was depressed.

It's been over a year, and the pain of my loss is still there. I tell myself not to think about it, but the reality is that I think about it every day yet. I tried going to the support group at the hospital, but I was very uncomfortable there. I have a hard time expressing feelings and even more so in a group setting. So mostly, I share my feelings with Sue. I feel safe to cry with her. The consensus is that the death of a child tears couples apart; it's actually brought Sue and me closer together.

This tragedy with Jake has opened up my whole family—my parents and all six brothers and sisters. It really brought our family together. I never saw my dad cry before but he sure was crying with all of us at the hospital and the funeral. We learned it's okay to cry, and it's okay to hug each other. Since Jake died, I actually hugged my dad, mom, sisters, and brothers. Had I known how wonderful it feels, I would have done it a long time ago. It took Jake's passing to open up all of us.

When it first happened, I kept asking, "Why, God? What could I have done to prevent this tragedy? What did I do? God, are you punishing me for something?" I figured there must have been something I did wrong, but I couldn't think of anything I did that was that bad. I went through weeks of questioning before I started to realize it wasn't anything we did or did not do. It helped me a lot when our priest told us that God doesn't punish people.

Over time, Jake's death brought me closer to God. I believe in God now even more than I did. In fact, now I say, "There really is a God. God is my lifeline to Jake. I think God is taking care of him up in heaven." When I see clouds in the sky, I think of him up there, and he's wrapped in a puffy, white cloud blanket. Before, I didn't believe in life after death. I almost have to now. I often feel like

Jake is right here, and I carry on a conversation with him. I get vibes, so to speak.

Steve has awakened to the possibility of life after death because he experiences Jake as right here. In addition to his own experiences, he is well aware of the numerous signs and messages that Sue and others receive from Jake's spirit. Steve continued to describe his spiritual transformation.

Since Jake's death, I've come to believe in angels. Before it was more fictional—like a nice story you tell little kids. Now angels are real to me. I know Jake is an angel, and he's up there in heaven watching over the animals, as well as our whole family.

I also pray more since Jake's death. I ask God, "Please take care of Jake and watch over him." During our second pregnancy, I prayed every day, "Please give us a healthy baby boy or baby girl." After what happened with Jake, I no longer have this naïve bliss about pregnancy.

The "Why" Questions

Sue, like Steve, went through a period of asking the "why" questions. During our interview, Sue talked about a very big shift she experienced concerning this issue. She began her journey asking the age-old questions, "Why, God? Why did this have to happen? Why did Jake have to die?" At nineteen months along her healing journey, Sue said:

I have stopped asking, "Why?" I trust he was here for a reason, and he fulfilled that reason even if I don't know what it is. Someday I may find out. That someday might not be until I die, and that's okay. Now I say to myself, "He died. It happened. It doesn't matter why. Now it's just important for me to know he's right here with me in spirit as I continue on with my life."

I feel sorry for people who don't believe in life after death. If you don't believe, then life is just a waste. I know deep in my heart that Jacob is alive and talking to me from heaven. It helps me to know that his life goes on.

Another Dream About Jake With the Animals

As Sue went about her daily life, she often found herself thinking about all the spirit communication from Jake. She was especially intrigued with Jake's ability to come into people's dreams—both her own dreams and those of her friends. Six months after receiving Dr. Kate's letter, Sue received another letter from a fellow animal-lover who also had a dream about Jacob. Denise wrote:

Dear Sue:

I went to bed one night last week really depressed. I've been missing my dog Rajza terribly ever since she died. That night I had a dream about her, and I want to share it with you.

First, I need to explain that Rajza had a habit of barking right after we turned out all the lights and crawled into bed. After she quieted down, I would say, "Goodnight, Rajza girl," and she would lie down and go to sleep. In this dream, I heard a series of barks like Rajza used to do each night. I looked, and there in the middle of a field stood a little boy with dirty blond hair. He had my three dogs with him, Rajza, Vixen, and Cinnamon.

He said to me, "Rajza wanted me to tell you that she is okay." I was crying as I looked around in awe. There were SO MANY animals with the boy. I looked back at him and said, "Thank you." He smiled and simply said, "Yeah," and turned to leave.

He has your smile, Sue. It was him! It was Jake! I know it in my heart. I hollered after him to wait. He turned and kind of quirked his eyebrow. I asked him to tell my dogs that I miss them and love them so much. Again, he smiled and said, "They know." He was gone then. Rajza and Vixen both looked at me and turned to follow Jake. Cinnamon was hot on their heels. All the other animals just kind of disappeared. I was alone then, but my heart was at ease. I'm so grateful to know that Rajza is okay.

Love and prayers, Denise

Jake and the Spirit Animals

There seems to be a great deal of evidence that Jacob's spirit is taking care of spirit animals on the other side. Could this really be true? Yes, I do believe it's true. It's no accident that so many different people gave Sue a message about Jake taking care of animals. This repetitive theme came from Xena with her puppy balloons; the spiritual medium who reported seeing Jake and Butch together; Dr. Kate, who dreamed of Jake playing with a puppy in heaven; Sue, who found a picture of Jacob on the cover of *All God's Creatures Go To Heaven*; and Denise, who dreamed of Jake surrounded with animals in heaven.

A soul taking care of the spirit animals on the other side was not a new idea to me. In 1992, a dear client named Margaret died of cancer, and then her spirit spoke to me through Roy Waite, a spiritual medium, for one hour each month for two years. Her soul purpose is to bring the world this message: *"There is no death, and life on the other side is a fun adventure."* She had much to say about a special place on the other side she called the "Animal Kingdom." It's a place where all the wild animals and pets live peacefully together.

According to Margaret, there are certain souls who volunteer to work in this kingdom. These souls have a deep love for all God's creatures and spend their time in heaven healing and loving the spirit animals. When these souls are born here on earth, they bring this deep love with them. As children, they bring home strays and beg to have a pet; then, as adults, they might care for many pets or choose to become zookeepers, animal trainers, or veterinarians. They may volunteer at shelters or work for animal rights groups. These souls are the animal lovers of the world, and they usually live their purpose with passion.

All these reports about Jacob being with the spirit animals led me to conclude that Jacob is one of those souls who dedicates his time and energy to working in the "Animal Kingdom." Sue also describes herself as an animal lover. It seems natural that Jake would come to a mother who is a like-minded soul and also has a strong heart connection with her beloved pets.

I Can Laugh Again

During our first interview, just nineteen months after Jake's transition, Sue cried a bit here and there as she told the story of her healing journey. The amazing thing was that she spent a lot of time laughing. She laughed with great delight as she described Jake's first birthday party and her joyful experiences of spirit communication from her son. Her laughter was genuine and refreshing; she was actually joyful telling me her stories. I took it as a sign that she had indeed moved through the original gripping pain of her grief. In fact, she said exactly that.

> *I have done so much to heal my grief. I have expressed my pain over and over to anyone who would listen. I have wailed, screamed out my anger, bargained with God, written in my journal, attended support groups, seen a grief counselor, and even created a beautiful memory book about Jacob's birth and death. I forced myself to do the difficult things because I needed to, for me.*

At some point, I noticed I was on the other side of the deep grief. I could laugh again and enjoy small amounts of time without crying. I think I moved through the stages of grief rather quickly because I just kept releasing the pain.

I will always have some sadness in my heart about Jake. The intense pain goes away, but there's always a bittersweet feeling. It's like missing something you want but don't have. However, I filled the hole in my heart with love, and ninety percent of the time, I focus on the love.

Sue continues to create ways to feel joyful while she celebrates Jake's ongoing existence in spirit. Jake's first birthday party with family members created so much healing that Sue decided to make it an annual event. Close friends heard about it and asked to be included. Before Jake's second birthday, Sue sent out this announcement:

You are invited to our annual summer cookout in memory of Jake. Bring balloons, confetti, and streamers. We will be releasing balloons to heaven again and blowing bubbles in his memory.

Forty people showed up for Jake's second birthday party. Sue looked amazed and delighted as she said to me, "My friends and family get the idea that Jake still exists. There's a lot of joy in that!"

Keeping the Love Alive

Much of Jacob's story is a mystery that our logical human minds cannot fathom. With great wisdom, Sue has moved beyond the need for explanations about the many mysteries surrounding Jake. She believes his spirit has the ability to appear in dreams and send messages to her through the veil. She doesn't question why or how—she just takes in the love from her son each time he comes. For her it's not about mind or making sense—it's about heart. Sue knows in her heart. She put it very simply, "I just believe."

From the moment Jake died, Sue made a commitment to keep her love for him alive. She does all kinds of things to attain this goal. She explained.

I think of Jake's spirit as being right here with us. I continue to do things for Jake to recognize him as part of the family. If I see a mug or a toy with "Jake" written on it, I buy it. I put his picture in a locket that I always wear around my neck. I feel naked without it. Each night I kiss his picture good night and say, "I love you, Jake."

It bothers me if I forget, just like it would bother me if he was here in the physical, and I forgot to kiss my son good night.

I'm keeping the love alive by doing these things. The love I have for Jake is always there even if I forget sometimes. I want to keep nurturing the love, so my connection to him stays strong. It's very easy for me to just do these things. Jake came to learn love and teach love, so I'm doing my part to keep the love alive.

Angel Bears for Healing

Sue felt inspired to find a little bear that she could hold and hug when she was missing Jake. It had to be just the right kind of bear. She searched and searched with no success. Then she found a baby-blue bear with angel wings—and the wings had sparkles! She knew immediately this was her "Jake Bear."

The angel bear is a symbol of Jake's spirit, so Sue likes to have the Jake Bear in their family pictures. Whenever they have a family portrait taken, somebody holds the bear. They took Chad's one-year Christmas photo on a rocking horse and put the baby-blue angel bear down on the rocker. Sue declared, "Jake is still part of our family, but it's hard to get a photo of a spirit. I get a warm, cozy feeling in my heart when I see the Jake Bear in our pictures. It's a reminder that he is indeed still with us."

Sue also started a ritual of giving teddy bears with angel wings to other parents who had lost a baby or child; she delivers them right before the baby's first birthday. If it was a boy, she gives the parents a baby-blue bear; if it was a girl, they receive a pink bear with white wings. Sue thinks the angel bears are a perfect symbol for a baby's spirit. She says to the parents, "Here's a little gift in memory of your baby. Because you're sad, you might need something to hug sometimes. You can wrap your arms around this bear when you have an urge to snuggle with your baby. I hug my Jake Bear, and I always feel better."

Guidance to Find the Perfect Gift

Sue believes it is part of her purpose to extend herself to many mothers who have lost a baby or a child. She has a very generous heart, so she gives both time and energy to help these women, often providing support through long phone conversations. This is not a burden for Sue; in fact, she receives a great deal of joy from these conversations. Sue explained.

I feel so fulfilled when I'm talking with these other mothers. I know providing this kind of support is part of my mission—my soul work. I have great heart connections with these women. Some become like family to me.

Sue often gives gifts to these mothers to commemorate special occasions like birthdays, Valentine's Day, or Mother's Day. Of course, each time it has to be the perfect gift. For Sue, this means she has to find something that has a special significance to the mother. These gifts are often very difficult to find. Sue is a busy career woman, wife, and mother, so she has very little time to shop. However, she has found a very innovative way to do her shopping—she simply asks for guidance from the spirit of the baby! This next story shows how easily this process works.

One woman from the infant loss support group lost a baby named Sophie. I wanted to get her a gift with her baby's name on it. Of course, all I could find were things inscribed with Sophia—with an "a" instead of an "e." Finally, I said, "Okay, Sophie, help me out here." I felt guided to go to my computer, log on to e-Bay, and type in "bear" and "Sophie." Within seconds, a beautiful Cherished Teddy inscribed with "Sophie" popped up on my computer screen! The auction was ending in minutes, so I just had time to make a bid. This was the last one and I got it! I absolutely know it was Sophie guiding me to this perfect gift. It was just so cool!

When Sue first started finding the perfect gift, she would say to the mother, "It was your baby who told me what to do." At first, she was just saying the words without really believing them herself. When it came to this issue, she didn't believe her own experience. Sue always trusted that she could get messages from Jake, but she just couldn't believe she was receiving guidance from the spirit of any other baby. This idea was just too far out there!

During one of our many interviews, I shared with Sue that I thought Jake and all the other babies in this book were giving me guidance as I wrote their stories. This conversation was a catalyst for a major change in Sue's belief system. Sue said:

I suddenly got it that these babies really are guiding me to find the perfect gifts. I'm just awed that this could be true! Believing this is a big shift for me. It's not that I see or hear anything specific. Rather, I just get inspired about where to look. Funny, I always find something wonderful if I just follow the thoughts that come into my mind. Maybe the babies are whispering to me because I'm the only one willing to listen.

Sue's Mission: Healing Grief After Infant Loss

Sue has a mission to help others deal with grief, and the first step in fulfilling this was to donate a camcorder to the NICU where Jake was born. The nurses call it "The Jake Cam." Sue and Steve received so much comfort from their video of Jake's time here on earth that they wanted other parents to have the same opportunity. Sue asked the nurses to use it when a baby is in crisis, knowing that the parents will be so grateful to have these precious moments recorded for all time.

Two years after Jake's death, Sue and Steve were invited to talk with residents and interns specializing in obstetrics training at the hospital where Jake was delivered. They spoke with thirty future doctors about their experience of losing Jake and their emotional needs as the parents of a dying baby. When they talked about their devastating heartbreak, these doctors looked shocked. It was an important moment.

Sue also brought Jake's memory book and had it on display in the back of the room. After the program, most of the doctors looked through it. Jake's story in pictures really touched their hearts. Many of them cried as they leafed through the album. One doctor commented, "This is incredible!"

Sue has since been invited to speak at a nursing school about the emotional needs of parents who have a baby in crisis. She was so well received that the staff invited her to return each year and tell Jake's story. Sue sees each of these speaking opportunities as a way to fulfill her mission of helping others understand the grief process. Each time she is dropping another pebble in the pool, and the circles of healing flow out.

People have always come to Sue to share their troubles and use her shoulder to cry on. Since Jake's transition, many people in grief are drawn to her compassionate heart. Sue simply relates what she's experienced on her healing journey.

I am now the leader for the infant loss support group at the hospital where Jake died. I love doing this work—in fact, it's not work, it's a joy to assist others in their healing. I keep saying to the new parents, "You have to get beyond the pain. It's not that you will ever get over your child, but you will get over the pain." Some people keep talking about their grief, and I can tell that they are stuck in it. I get the feeling they're hanging on to their pain instead of releasing it. I tell my story about dealing with Jake's death, and people really listen. I just tell them what I learned with Jake, and it seems to help.

Jake at Work Behind the Scenes

It's fascinating how Sue and Jake's story came to be in this book. It's another one of those mystical moments that abound in Jake's life. Five months after Jake's death, Sue was looking for a weight loss counselor because she had gained weight with her pregnancy and then gained even more during the first months of her grief. Sue belongs to a health club where Cole's Grandma Sandy works as a weight loss counselor. Sue had seen flyers about Sandy's lifestyle coaching sessions at the health club, but had never paid attention to them. After Jake's death, she went to the health club and saw Sandy's flyer again. This time she felt a strong urge to make an appointment.

During the first session, when Sue started talking about the stress of Jake's birth and death, Sandy shared that her grandson Cole was born at the same hospital and lived only twelve days. (See Chapter One.) In fact, Jake died five days after Cole. Sue described her sense of how this fated meeting with Sandy came to be.

I'm sure Cole and Jake brought us together. Of all the hundreds of weight loss counselors in Madison, I found Sandy. I'm sure Jake's spirit was inspiring me as I made the decision to ask for help. And he was also guiding me to respond to that flyer and pick Cole's grandmother to be my counselor. There's just no other way to explain this meant-to-be connection.

Funny, I had already met Cole's mother, Danita, at the hospital infant loss support group. I knew all about Cole's birth and that he only lived twelve days. Sandy and I were both awe-struck when we realized all of our connections.

Early in my healing journey, I kept seeing Jake's story in a book about healing grief. I held this vision in my heart but did not develop any plan to make it happen. A year later, Sandy called to say that Dr. Wesch was writing a book about healing grief after the loss of an infant. Sandy connected me with her, and the rest is history. I'm so grateful Spirit connected all of us.

It is truly amazing what's unfolded since I listened to that inspiration to make an appointment with Sandy. Of course, this was not an accident or a coincidence. I believe with all my heart that Jake and Cole engineered this connection to Sandy, who then connected me to a woman who could get my story out to the world. I feel very supported in my mission to help others heal from the loss of an infant.

Having Jake's story in this grief book is cool because this will teach so many more people. I'm sure many will be helped through their grief—people I'll never meet. Knowing this gives even greater purpose to Jacob's death.

Points to Ponder

When we look at Jake with human eyes only, he appears to be a tiny, helpless infant who lived only twenty-one hours and thirty-three minutes. However, when we look with soul eyes, a new image is revealed—that of a powerful spirit who is wise, humorous, joyous, and loving as he continues his eternal soul journey in the spirit world. Obviously, he has the power to pierce the veil so he can touch many people, open hearts, extend love, and inspire more love in the world. Like the Inca spirit babies, Jake brings powerful medicine to his family and all those connected to his birth and death.

There is a spiritual principle that says whatever you focus on gets bigger. Sue intuitively knows to focus on healing and indeed, healing does occur. She also keeps her attention on creating feelings of love, joy, and peace. Thus, within a year of Jake's passing, her heart is filled with these high-frequency feelings instead of sorrow.

Sue describes Jake's spirit as joyful and tells story after story of how his spirit invites her to laugh. Undeniably, one of the key elements of this mother's successful healing journey is her ability to focus on joy. She is uplifted each time she gets a sign from Jake and savors this feeling, thus keeping her heart clear of bitterness. Sue also shares her joy by telling everyone she knows about her messages from Jake and by inviting people to celebrate his memory at an annual party. Sue is jubilant about her own spiritual transformation and continuously shares this uplifting feeling with family and friends as she moves along her pathway to wholeness.

Sue's healing journey beautifully illustrates the four aspects of healing grief using Radiant Heart Healing: 1) release the pain, 2) fill your heart with love, 3) have a believable experience of spirit communication, and 4) shift to a spiritual perspective about life, death, and the afterlife. Sue did not have any information about Radiant Heart Healing while she was moving along on her healing journey. However, she completed each of the four steps in this process as if she were following a set of very explicit instructions. I find this quite amazing!

Notice that Sue spends hours and hours releasing her grief during the first year after Jake's death. She describes wailing when the doctors told her

Jake wouldn't make it, lying in bed crying for hours at a time the first weeks after Jake's funeral, and crying for months after his death as she talked about Jake to her family and friends. She truly did express her pain to anyone who would listen. Sue states, "I think I moved through the stages of grief rather quickly because I just kept releasing the pain."

After Jake's death, Sue feels very inspired to keep her love for Jake alive. Amazingly, she loves Jake's spirit with the same intensity that she loved Jake's physical self. Sue keeps her love alive with her numerous rituals: wearing Jake's picture in a locket, saying good night and kissing his picture before bed, honoring the memory of his birth with an annual celebration, and paying attention to all the signs and messages coming from his spirit. Sue also has an enormous sense of gratitude for the gift of Jake's life, both here and in the spirit world. Focusing on this feeling produces even more love.

In addition to filling her heart with love *for* Jake, Sue has intuitively found a way to fill her heart with love *from* Jake. These are very different processes. Sue receives love from Jake's powerful spirit whenever she senses his presence. Each time she gets some kind of sign from Jake or has a dream visitation, she is aware of experiencing more love and feels so very blessed to know their hearts are still connected. Sue's ability to receive love is a very significant component of her successful healing journey.

Sue begins getting believable messages from Jake's spirit within weeks of his funeral. Her first experience is hearing a child's voice say, "Mommy, don't cry. I don't like you crying." It's seems quite astonishing that this ordinary woman with no spiritual training could spontaneously hear her son speaking from the other side. I believe Sue's deep love for Jake and her longing to connect with him are the catalysts for her to open to this spiritual gift.

Within a year of Jake's death, Sue also recognizes she is receiving guidance and inspiration from other spirit babies, like Sophie. As the story unfolds, Sue's gift for communicating with spirit babies is obviously getting stronger. It will be fascinating to see how much this ability evolves as she continues to follow her heart and help other mothers heal their grief. *What will Sue be doing ten or even twenty years after Jake's transition? It's a very interesting question!*

At the end of this story, we see that Sue is well aware that she and Jake have a soul agreement to come together in the physical world, be separated at the human level through Jake's early death, and then reconnect at the soul level. Early in the story, Sue speaks of her mission to first heal her own heart and then to teach others about healing grief. As this book goes to press, approximately ten years after Jake's death, Sue is leading the infant loss support group at the hospital where Jacob died; and every year she speaks to both doctors and nurses about the needs of parents when their baby is dying in the hospital. This resilient young woman exudes both joy and passion as she fulfills her soul mission of helping others to heal after infant loss.

CHAPTER THREE

Awakening to Soul Love

Soul love is what David is all about. He's just pouring love out to you.
There's so much love it makes me cry. He says grab it and drink!
—Barbara, Messenger for David

After a tragic, early miscarriage, Judith silently carried the burden of guilt, shame, and deep grief for over forty years. All this time, she had no hope of finding relief for her broken heart. Then a synchronistic meeting opened a door—and she had the courage and the wisdom to say, "Yes!" to Spirit. This meeting arranged by Spirit became the catalyst for her to find a spiritual solution to her grief. Below is the story of Judith's transformational healing journey in her own words.

The Snowstorm

It all began with the Great Chicago Snow of 1967. Everyone who experienced it has a story about the record storm whose gusts of 53mph dumped over sixteen inches of snow during the afternoon rush hour. Leaving work, I battled my way through howling winds and stinging snow for over seven hours. My usual commuter train was barely moving, and I ended up riding a part of the way in a stranger's car, then trudging through deep snowdrifts for a mile. It was absolute chaos!

I finally arrived home close to midnight. By that time, there was a lull in the storm, and the landscape was absolutely still with the light of the moon on the fresh snow. The scene was so beautiful, so otherworldly, the air so refreshing that I decided to shovel off the walks and driveway. I felt very connected to God and to my soul in the silence of that moonlit night.

The next morning I started bleeding. When it didn't stop, I went to my doctor, who told me I was having a miscarriage. What a shock! My first child was only three months old, so it never dawned on me that I was pregnant. I was devastated! Intuitively, I knew it was a boy and named him David.

More Than Forty Years of Guilt, Shame, and Grief

My sister and I were born a year apart, and we were always close. My dream was that my first two children would come within a year of each other and share the same kind of relationship. But the baby I always dreamed of came and went before I knew of his existence. I was heartbroken and inconsolable! Of course, I blamed myself for the miscarriage, and for over forty years, in addition to my unhealed grief, I carried the weight of great unrelenting guilt and deep shame. These painful feelings were so pervasive they seemed to eat away at my soul.

For weeks after the miscarriage, I wanted to cry all the time. I tried to hold myself together and keep a stiff upper lip, but the tears flowed endlessly. My husband told me again and again to stop crying. One really difficult day I said to him, "I know you can't do anything; I just need you to hold me while I cry." When he couldn't, I felt even worse and so alone in my feelings.

I was elated a few months later to find that I was pregnant again—elated and apprehensive. What if I lost the last baby not because of shoveling snow, but because there was something wrong with me? Or had I been punished because I wasn't a good enough person? What if I lost this baby? Could I handle that? How could I ever look anyone in the eye again? And the due date was only a few days from the anniversary of my loss, yet another reminder of what had happened.

I went on an early pregnancy leave from work and took really good care of myself. Because I lived over an hour away from the hospital and because my first delivery was very fast, the doctor told me that when this third baby was ready, he would induce labor. A week before the due date and two days before the anniversary of my miscarriage, I went in for my usual appointment and was told to be at the hospital the next day.

When I first saw the doctor in the labor room, I remember saying to him, "This baby will come before midnight, won't it?" And again, "My baby will be here soon, right?" I couldn't actually say the words that were in my head; I felt too ashamed to bring up the miscarriage. I hoped that my doctor could hear the urgency in my voice and see in my records what had happened the year before. That he would realize how very important it was that this child have his own day. That if anything could be done to speed things up, he would do it. I wanted this baby's birthday to be one of joy. I didn't want a lifetime of celebrating this birth to be days tinged with my shame. In the delivery room, I kept my eye on the clock and thanked God when my son was born at 11:40 p.m. My precious, new son would have a day all his own.

Two years later we were blessed with another child—a sweet, strawberry blonde girl. How wonderful! Two sons and a daughter. Caring for three small children kept me very busy, so I was usually able to bury the pain about David. I rarely thought about him until the anniversary of my miscarriage loomed near; then all my heartache would return full force.

Depression Prevails

Once my little ones were all in school, I could no longer hide from my feelings; it became really obvious to me that I was seriously depressed. My life seemed empty and devoid of meaning. On some level, I knew there had to more to life—something richer and deeper than what I was experiencing. I had no idea what this could be.

My religion didn't seem to be helping. Raised a devout Catholic, I began to question everything. Is there a God? Maybe. Maybe not. I did everything I was supposed to do and look what's happened—my baby died anyway. During this time, I lost my faith.

I thought that if I could get rid of my depression I could find out what was missing from my life. So I set out on a quest to overcome my despondency. I was in and out of counseling for fifteen years or so, and even though I saw several different professionals, nothing seemed to help. During this time, my husband and I divorced, and fifteen years later I remarried. It didn't seem to matter if I was married or single, I was still depressed.

Strangely, I never associated my depression with the miscarriage. I talked about David to one therapist, but nothing changed. One of my counselors taught me to use imagery to work with my inner child. In retrospect, this was the most helpful technique I learned in therapy. I seem to have a natural gift for becoming very relaxed and allowing spontaneous images to come into my mind—it's a bit like daydreaming. Somehow, these positive images brought some relief, but it didn't last.

I devoured self-help books and found I was drawn to those with a spiritual bent. My search led me to the exploration of world religions, even attending the Church of Religious Science for a time, and going to the Theosophical Society for lectures and seminars. However, nothing really seemed to help.

After all this effort, I was still very depressed, so I concluded there was nothing more I could do. I decided I'd just have to live with my despair and keep it hidden. I believed my depression would be with me until the grave. There was no way out.

A Dream Visitation

Thirty-eight years after the miscarriage, I had a vivid dream. A group of friends and I were touring through ancient Greece. We were having such a wonderful time—everyone was happy and excited to be sightseeing. We were walking through the countryside, when over the hill came three young men in short, white togas and sandals. They were all laughing and enjoying one another's company. Then this handsome young man stepped out of the trio, looked at me, and said, "Don't worry about it. I'm fine. Have a good time." Somehow I knew it was David, my spirit baby, even though he presented himself as a grown man.

The dream brought me a few moments of wonder and joy. For the first time, I considered the possibility that my son still exists, but in spirit form, and that he's happy where he is. I also started thinking, "The way things turned out was the way things were supposed to turn out." I was happy for a short time, but I couldn't hold on to the feeling. Eventually I began to doubt the experience. I kept asking myself, "Did I make up this dream? Was it just wishful thinking?" I soon told myself that I had just imagined it in order to feel better. Gradually, I slid back into my negative feelings and pushed them deep within.

The Depths of Despair

My stepson and his wife live on the other side of the country. About a year after this dream, she had a miscarriage. Suddenly everything that was unhealed came to the surface—all my grief was in my face. My pain paralyzed me, and even though I wanted to wrap my arms around her and offer comfort, I found myself totally incapacitated. I couldn't even pick up the phone.

The guilt and shame about my miscarriage were compounded by my inability to console my stepdaughter. I hated my weakness. My self-esteem hit rock bottom! My grief took me to the depths of despair once again, without a ray of hope for climbing out of this dark place. It was one of the lowest points of my life.

A Meant-to-Be Connection

I carried these intense, shameful feelings for over a year, feeling immobilized, not knowing what to do. Then I met Dr. Wesch at a spiritual networking group. She introduced herself as an author and said she was writing a book about healing grief after the loss of an infant. I felt such hope! Maybe I could find some relief. These words tumbled out, "I had a miscarriage forty years ago, and next week is the anniversary." I burst into tears, and was shocked to be crying so hard in public. I was terribly embarrassed.

Dr. Wesch invited me to do an interview for her book and participate in some Radiant Heart Healing sessions. My heart said yes without needing more information. I intuitively knew this was one of those meant-to-be connections.

During the first session, I cried and cried while sharing the tragedy of my second pregnancy. Then we did some simple Radiant Heart Healing visualizations to clear the energy of grief. It worked! I could actually feel the pain flowing not just from my heart, but from my whole body! Immediately, I could breathe more easily—like a constriction had been released.

Then this amazing thing happened. In my mind's eye, a transparent ball of sparkling light appeared right in front of me; I could see through it. I announced: "My son is right here. He's a shimmering ball of energy. I can feel our connection. There's a ray of energy coming into my heart from the ball. I feel this great love coming from him to me. I feel his happiness for me, and his words are coming to me. He's saying, 'I'm happy, Mom. I'm so proud of you for doing this healing! I'm so proud. Good for you!'"

Afterwards, I sat in wonder. In the quiet, I became aware of this blue energy surrounding me like an aqua shawl around my shoulders. My mind went back in time to the nativity set we had when I was a child. The color that I saw around me was the same shade of blue that Mother Mary wore. It was a moment of deep spiritual comfort.

This healing session touched me deeply, and I was filled with gratitude that my spirit son appeared and sent such powerful love energy into my heart. He gave me such a wondrous gift that day. He is my healer. And what a powerful healer he is!

A Shift in Consciousness

After several more Radiant Heart Healing sessions, I felt like a totally different person. In only three sessions the grief, shame, and guilt associated with my miscarriage were completely released with this energy work. Dr. Wesch explained that all of my emotional pain was composed of negative energy that was stuck in the cells of my body, my emotional heart, and my aura. After clearing this heavy energy, the heartache I carried for all those years was simply gone.

When my whole being was filled with emotional pain, the word "miscarriage" always triggered very negative thoughts. Although the doctors assured me it wasn't my fault, just hearing that word brought up these self-judgments:

- *"I let my baby die."*
- *"There's something wrong with me."*
- *"I'm not good enough."*
- *"I'm not a good mother."*
- *"I couldn't keep the baby in me."*

I carried these dreadful thoughts for more than forty years, believing the whole time that I deserved to suffer. I even felt like God was punishing me because I was bad somehow. It never even occurred to me to pray for relief. I guess I didn't even realize that relief was possible.

I also believed I really shouldn't get over my grief about my miscarried baby—or any other loved ones, for that matter. These statements always seemed true to me:

- *"I'm dishonoring my baby if I'm not grieving."*
- *"Staying in grief means I really do love him."*
- *"Giving up grief means I don't love him."*

After releasing the energy of my painful feelings, I've changed my beliefs about David and my grief. This mental shift is really a miracle! It's very strange, but I no longer think of myself as having had a miscarriage. That's not how I see it anymore. These are my new beliefs: Now I have a relationship with my spirit baby, so I have gained a child, not lost one. My spirit son is happy where he is, and he wants me to be happy. He wants me to stop grieving and be at peace.

This new view of the situation has allowed me to be finished with my heartache. Now I see the whole experience with David as a blessing—a gift from my son. My spirit baby loves me dearly and wants me to know that he's always here for me. Because he and I have "met," I now believe:

- *"David came to point the way for my spiritual awakening."*
- *"He came to open up the unseen world to me."*
- *"This baby came to show me that I've always had a connection to the divine."*

I'm so grateful to David for this gift. It's so wonderful to transform my thoughts about this event that happened so many years ago. It's really a positive thing—my whole being is empowered, uplifted. I can do so much more with my life now that I'm free of the old, negative beliefs that kept me feeling like a powerless victim who had to suffer.

When I told Dr. Wesch my new thoughts about David and my miscarriage, she explained:

> *You've had a major shift in consciousness. You're now viewing your miscarriage experience with soul eyes, or eyes of love. Opening to this new perspective is the miracle of healing! Now that you've shifted your perspective, you can discover the gifts in this tragedy and find new meaning in your life. You're now free to heal at a much deeper level.*
>
> *This shift seems magical and out-of-the-blue. However, you've been preparing for this moment for a very long time. Don't forget you've had forty years of reading self-help books, going to therapy, and being a spiritual seeker. Everything you've learned came together in this defining moment! Now I believe you'll be forever changed.*

I know this is true because my thoughts before this shift in consciousness seem like those of a stranger. Sometimes I think, "Who was that woman who saw the miscarriage in such a negative way? I don't even know her anymore."

Now my heart feels lighter, and I'm at peace. I can hardly believe it! Doing energy work was the key to my healing. It's very strange, but I can't even quite remember how it felt to be so full of pain. It's been the most amazing experience!

Spontaneous Healing Visions

My healing continues even though I haven't had any more Radiant Heart Healing sessions. Whenever I allow myself time to relax and tune into the spirit world, I get these spontaneous healing visions. It's rather strange how it happens. I get calm and these wonderful pictures start coming, like a video playing in my mind with everything in magnificent colors.

Years ago, one of my therapists taught me to do healing visualizations with my inner child. When I first started this imagery work, I would see my little girl living in a coal bin with rickety furniture and no light. It was a pretty dismal picture! Gradually, as my depression improved somewhat, I began to see my little girl in brighter places.

After completing the Radiant Heart sessions, I had a wonderful daydream about my inner child. At first, I purposely imagined her playing in a beautiful garden. She was dressed in fancy Easter clothes and was playing and running through the flowers. She looked like a little lady in her ruffled dress, white shoes, and ribbons in her hair. I was so happy watching her in my mind's eye.

Then my daydream took on a life of its own. David spontaneously appeared. He too was dressed for Easter—little short pants and a matching jacket. So adorable! Then my inner child and David were no longer in a garden, but in a great field of flowers. The blooms were waist-high, and the children were having such fun, scampering about in this unlimited space. Freedom and delight filled these scenes. Remembering this vision of my little girl playing with my spirit son brings me so much joy!

I've also had several spontaneous visions of Miranda, my great-niece who was stillborn thirty years after I miscarried David. One was very brief, but so real. There was Miranda just walking away from me. She turned around and looked at me for just a moment. Then she smiled, waved, and went off to play. She had this shy, little smile. I could tell she was very happy.

Another time, while meditating, I found myself "up there" in the hills and the flowers. The fields were very open, and in the distance I could see rolling hills of gold, like California in the summertime. David and Miranda were running through the fields among fawns, bunnies, and butterflies. The children were playing, laughing, and filled with great joy. They came towards me, sat down under a tree to pet a fawn, and then got up and ran off again, laughing. It was obvious they loved being together.

My little dog, Chloe, was also in this vision, playing with the kids on the other side. It was the strangest thing! I would never have made that up!

Chloe is still alive and well, and was sleeping on the porch when this vision flowed into my mind. A psychic once told me that the spirits of animal companions have the ability to leave and visit the other side while they sleep. It's just like people who visit loved ones in the afterlife while they're asleep. Chloe loves children and loves to play with them. It looks like she also enjoys playing with the spirit babies.

I've come to believe that David is inspiring these daydreams. Here is how I think about the visions that come. Things happen in my visions that I wouldn't think to create, so it's not me generating these scenes. I really am tapping into another place. My son and Miranda have invited me into their world. They are giving me these precious gifts. They want me to open my heart and be joyful like they are. Holding these thoughts brings joy to my heart. These spontaneous visions are the moments that feed my soul!

On another day, I saw my spirit son become a wise old man. He got very tall and just morphed into a man with all the wisdom in the world. He announced, "I'm here for you. I'm going to show you the way." This was a spontaneous happening—certainly nothing I planned. So I guess he's trying to tell me that he's one of my spirit guides. I like that idea; it's comforting to think of him as a very wise being who's guiding my life.

Soul Love

I belong to a spiritual healing group, and one of the members, Barb, is a natural clairvoyant. As a child, she could see spirits and have conversations with them. During one of our meetings, Barb volunteered to connect with David and give me some messages. Here are her words:

Your son David is here. He's showing himself as a gorgeous, robust young man with brown hair and blue eyes. He's giving me an image of you reading a book. He wants you to really read that book and be a part of that, to live that book. Soul love is what he's about.

He loves you. There's just such a huge amount of love! He is just pouring out love to you. There is so much love it makes me cry. He says grab it and drink! Whenever I talk to spirits, they hold out a lot of love.

He is one of your guides. You talk to him a lot. He understands. He knows when you're thinking of him and asking for guidance. He hears you. He safeguards you with a protective wall. He says, "I'm always pushing you. Do you feel that push? It's me." He's raising his hand. When you feel that, remember he is guiding you.

He says you're here to be a teacher. Teaching is the way to go. Be the role model. You're already doing it, and you're meant to be that in the future in a significant way. He's very big on this role model thing.

He wants you to show other women that you healed from the anguish you felt after the miscarriage. Be a model for them. Show them what they can do to pull themselves up by their bootstraps. He shows you pulling them up. You are to encourage other women to come through the healing process. Your mission is to help them heal from the guilt, the shame, and the grief of losing a baby.

These messages from my spirit son absolutely blew me away! Barb had no idea that I sat in my car before group, reading a book by Sanaya Roman entitled *Soul Love*. It's amazing to me that my son gave me a message about the same topic. It was really quite eerie! In retrospect, I felt something was really pushing me to buy the book that afternoon as I browsed through the bookstore. David's message from Barb is a gift I will always treasure. And I will hold her words in my mind and my son's love in my heart forever.

Immediately after this reading, I felt inspired to ask David to give me a message directly. Barb and the rest of the group watched in respectful silence as I retrieved the book from my purse and opened it randomly. My gaze was magnetically drawn to these words, "Evolve and expand your love through soul contact." That is exactly what David wants me to do! And we're doing it together!

Feeling David's Presence

Several weeks ago, I had a very interesting sensation at my back. I felt a semicircle of soft energy behind me, like I had backed into a wall made of a down quilt that was two feet thick. It seemed like this quilt was wrapping around me in a big, soft hug. It was really big—like "stretch out my arms" big. When it happened, I thought, "David." Intuitively I knew it was my son's energetic presence.

It's happened several times since then, and each time I get this warm glow in my heart and feel very loved. A trusted psychic confirmed that this sensation of being wrapped in a huge down quilt is coming from David. She explained:

When your spirit son comes close, he raises your vibration with his energy. What you feel is your own aura that has been intensified by David's love. Your son is giving you a big "aura hug!"

That's such a cool thought! I believe her. I wish I could see my aura too—it must be especially big and bright when David comes close.

There are still times that I doubt my spiritual experiences, but David's presence reminds me that I really do have access to the spirit world. Each time I feel him with me, I'm encouraged to keep doing whatever I can to continue connecting with the angels, my guides, and my loved ones on the other side.

Being Lifted Up

One morning I was alone in my living room reading a spiritual book; music that especially touches my heart was playing in the background. Suddenly, my awareness shifted from this physical world, and I found myself transported into the spirit realm.

David and thirty or forty spirit ancestors formed a semi-circle behind me. Sensing their love and presence was so overwhelming that tears of awe flowed down my face. Everything was just so beautiful, so perfect.

My spirit family seemed to be showing me a huge, wide vista. The way was totally clear, as if they wanted me to see into forever. The vision kept unfolding in my mind like a video. First, I was lying down while all my celestial ancestors and David held me aloft. Operating as a unit, we all rose up into the heavens, where they set me upright. There I was with my feet planted firmly on a path of gold—it was very straight and very narrow.

On both sides of this golden path, puffy little clouds hung in midair, but as I walked, these clouds turned into thousands of spirit guides. They were misty, so I could see right through them. My ancestors and David soon joined this huge assembly. It seemed as if they were all gathered in a big amphitheater to witness a special event.

Divine love flowed everywhere, and a sacred hush covered the scene. Great peace and serenity washed over me. With each step, I could feel their encouragement and happiness for me. They were saying, "We're glad you're finally here. This is where you are meant to be."

I continued walking down the golden path towards a great light in the distance. I couldn't look directly at it, but somehow I knew it was there. I got close to the edge of the light rays and knew that this was all the farther I was supposed to go; I turned and began retracing my steps.

Suddenly I woke from this spiritual vision and found myself back in my living room. David and my spirit ancestors were still with me, and I felt them giving me a loving aura hug. For some time, I remained quiet, totally immersed in the vibrations of peace and serenity. I was in touch with the sacredness of my being. For those brief moments, I felt my soul!

Intuitively, I know David inspired this experience—it was his way of saying, "You're on the right path, Mom. Keep going forward! I'm here encouraging you every step of the way." Although my journey on the golden path lasted only ten minutes, its imagery was rich with significance.

Something More

Since my shift in consciousness, I'm beginning to realize that my disconnection from Spirit has been a big factor in my life-long depression. For years now, I've had a feeling there was something more to life, but I just couldn't grasp it. There was the knowing, the wanting, and the yearning—and then nothing. I couldn't find the something more and I didn't know how to reach it.

After my miscarriage, I didn't have a longing to connect with my son because it never occurred to me that a miscarried baby has a spirit that exists in the afterlife. After thirty-eight years, David's dream visitation was the first inkling that my spirit son exists somewhere. The dream was memorable, but I didn't really know what to make of it, so it was not a moment of spiritual awakening for me.

I used to read spiritual books and think: *That works for other people but not me. If I were meant to be in that arena, I would be there. The ability to connect with angels and deceased loved ones is a gift—you are born with it or you are not. Since I don't have the gift, there's nothing there for me.*

Now, using my soul eyes, everything looks different. I've discovered connecting with loved ones on the other side is a skill that can be learned— all you need is desire, some instruction, patience, and a quiet place to meditate. I intend to keep reading spiritual books and taking classes to develop my intuition, so I can bond in a deeper way with my spirit son.

I've also come to understand that my connection to David is my entry to the whole spiritual realm. This is the most wonderful blessing of my journey through grief! After all those years of yearning, finally, I have an amazing, new life. *I have found the something more!*

My healing journey took forty years, but that doesn't matter. My spirit son has been waiting all this time to share his love. It's not too late for me!

Points to Ponder

At first glance, it looks like Judith magically heals forty years of pain in her first Radiant Heart Healing session. What happened that allowed this "magic" to occur?

At the beginning of our first session, Judith's heart is filled with the negative energy of guilt, shame, and grief; and all this negative energy acts as a very thick, yet invisible, barrier to the love her spirit son is always sending. Doing the Radiant Heart release visualizations removes this energetic barrier and allows the soul love from David to flow easily into his mother's heart. This influx of soul love is very uplifting for Judith; at the same time, it opens her soul eyes so she can "see" her spirit son as a shimmering ball of energy and receive both his love and his words. This experience of spirit contact creates a spontaneous healing that occurs in seconds without any effort from this grieving mother or me. It is a *fait accompli*, if you will.

So Judith's healing isn't magic after all. It's simply a clear demonstration of these words of wisdom: *Love is the most powerful healing force in the universe*. In addition, Judith began her healing journey a long time before we met; all the years of searching for something to heal her depression laid the groundwork for this defining moment.

David, like the Inca spirit babies, is a powerful healer for his mother as he guides her visions of the afterlife and brightens her aura with his soul love. With the loving guidance of her spirit son, Judith connects with her own soul light and establishes a direct link to divine love in the spiritual realm. After shifting her consciousness, this courageous woman is able to discover the "something more" about life—it's a connection to divine love! Making this connection changes everything! And it is available to all!

Judith's experience of long-term, buried guilt, shame, and grief is shared by millions of women in our culture who have miscarried a baby and silently bear this burden. Are you one of these women? If so, this story carries an important message for you: *It's never too late to heal.*

CHAPTER FOUR

❧❦❧

Our Souls Are
Connected for All Time

It is time for me to let you know I have never left you.
You have now opened your mind and heart to allow this communication.
My love never left you—you just couldn't feel it.
—Gregory, A Message for His Mother

Mary was only nineteen when she closed off her heart to avoid her grief after the tragic death of her first-born son. Twenty-six years passed before a diagnosis of cancer became the catalyst for this courageous mother to open her heart to forgiveness and healing. Here is Mary's story in her own words.

A Long Journey

I am now filled with pure joy whenever I think of my infant son Gregory! Of course, this wasn't always so. Gregory lived only a few days after we brought him home from the hospital. That fateful Sunday morning, he just stopped breathing; in a panic, we rushed him to the emergency room, where he died in my arms. The autopsy report showed he was born with a congenital heart condition. My grief was so intense that I simply shut down—I didn't even share my heartache with my husband or my family.

Many years passed before I dealt with my son's death; it was just too painful and overwhelming. My buried grief created a shield around my heart that protected me from my pain; however, this shield also kept me from feeling any joy or love. So I went through life feeling completely numb and thinking that was normal.

Twenty-six years after Gregory's death, a diagnosis of lymphoma was my wake-up call. The shock of this diagnosis ignited a strong will to live that pushed me to leave no stone unturned on my healing journey. The thought kept coming into my mind to focus on my spirituality. To achieve this goal, I sold my business, secluded myself, and spent hours every day meditating, journaling, breathing deeply, and releasing buried emotions. Only then did I face my grief of losing my first-born child.

A Rush of Hot Energy

The meditation ritual I used was very easy to do. First I lit candles on the little altar I created at home. Then I raised my hands to the heavens in a yoga salutation, saying, "Open my mind and heart to receive the goodness of God." Next, I breathed from my heart center for approximately fifteen minutes while sitting in front of my altar. During this silence, I kept my focus on the divine love energy that filled my whole chest, and usually went into a state of bliss!

Learning to meditate provided the opening for a connection with my son. The first inkling I had that something unusual was taking place was that my hands sometimes got extremely warm when I did the deep breathing. For months, I felt these physical sensations, but didn't know what was going on. I was so clueless back then! Eventually, it dawned on me that when thoughts of Gregory came to mind, my hands would get this rush of hot energy. It was such a thrill to recognize my son's energetic presence! Each time, my heart filled with such peace, and I would go about my day knowing I was connected to Gregory's spirit in heaven.

I didn't understand how this could be; yet, I found these experiences very intriguing, quite exciting, and extremely healing. Some time later, a holistic healer explained that it's very common for people to sense spirit energies when their vibration raises during meditation. Incidentally, I had to be in a meditative state to sense my son's presence; if I was busy, I didn't notice him even though I believe he was and still is always around me.

My ability to perceive spirit energy and receive communications from Gregory gradually became stronger. For years, the only thing I got was feeling the heat in my hands. I was content with this—it never occurred to me to ask for more. Then, I became more sensitive and could actually feel Gregory's presence in my space—just like I could feel any human being who walked into the room when my eyes were closed. My heart filled with pure joy and wonder each time I thought of how my loving son is in heaven, yet right here with me!

More years passed, and I expanded my abilities yet again and felt our hearts meld when I filled up with spirit love during my meditations. I felt doubly blessed—not only was Gregory coming to me, but I understood that he chose me to be his mother.

Then one day, I heard him say, "Hi, Mom." These words came through my spiritual hearing, and it was such a joy to actually get words! Then, gradually more and more words came into my mind. Eventually, I learned to take dictation from my spirit son—it's called automatic writing. Getting so many words filled my heart with even greater joy!

Using automatic writing, I allowed Gregory to channel his thoughts directly to me as I wrote them on a pad of paper. One of his first messages was quite a surprise.

> *Mom, I don't need you to communicate with me. I guide you whether we talk or not. Your soul and mine are connected for all time, and we are communicating whether you are conscious of this or not.*

After hearing this message, I realized that I was continually receiving his support and guidance without going into meditation and asking officially. I often went to bed thinking about a problem and woke up with an inspired solution. It never before occurred to me that my spirit son could be helping me solve my life problems while I slept. I loved knowing this—I felt very blessed to have his assistance

In another meditation session, I asked Gregory why it took me so long to connect with him as a spirit. Here is his answer.

> *It is time for me to let you know I have never left you. You have now opened your mind and heart to allow this communication. When you are closed, no one, not even a spirit, can penetrate. You loved no one—not even yourself. Through your fear of dying, you became soft again, and the shell of pain melted so that you could feel my love. My love never left you—you just couldn't feel it.*
>
> *When you healed your emotional pain, you opened your heart so that you could feel my energy. Joy resulted, and you were healed from the pain and forgave both yourself and me. You must stay in joy to serve the world. When you are in unhappy situations, you are blocked to the possibilities.*

Gregory's words of wisdom amazed me and lifted me to even higher levels of consciousness.

Gregory Opened the Door to the Spirit Word

It took me years to comprehend that Gregory left this physical world so he could be a spirit guide and angel for me. It was my son who opened the door to the spirit world. Since our initial connection ten years ago, he's brought Christ, Mother Mary, Buddha, other ascended masters, two angels named Chloe and Anastasia, and a spirit guide named Bridget. Recently, Gregory inspired me to begin working with Doreen Virtue's angel cards, so now I'm connected to a whole group of Archangels. I just love how he keeps helping me expand!

In my daily meditation, I often asked Gregory or various guides and angels for spiritual guidance. Sometimes I asked a question and then got my answer by drawing an angel card or opening a spiritual book at random and reading the message. Other times, I asked a question and wrote the inspirations in my journal. All of these techniques worked best after filling my heart with divine love, because then my vibration was really high, and I got a better connection to my son's spirit, as well as all my other guides and angels.

Forgiveness Through Grace

Grace is a gift from God, a healing from Spirit, if you will. Believing Gregory's congenital defects were my fault created deep feelings of guilt and shame. From the beginning I blamed myself, yet never understood exactly how I had caused this terrible tragedy.

For years after my diagnosis of cancer, I spent hours each week journaling to clear all my negative feelings, all the while knowing Gregory was close by and guiding me. Writing my thoughts brought me clarity and allowed me to release my guilt, give up my self-judgments, and develop a deep sense of compassion for the young mother I was so long ago. Finally, I moved from my head to my heart and came to know I was not to blame for anything. Rather, his passing was part of the divine plan. Connecting with Gregory's spirit created a bridge for the energy of forgiveness to flow into my heart—it felt like grace.

Sometimes the best we can do is to pray and give our problems to God and the angels. My spiritual quest brought me this wisdom, "I am a human being, and as a human I don't have to do everything myself." I've also learned forgiveness is not a one-time thing; rather, it's a journey of many forward steps, all requiring great courage. Getting to the peace of forgiveness made every step worth the effort.

Before turning things over to God and the angels, I did the work that needed to be done at the human level. This work included setting an intention, collecting information by reading, and then moving into my meditation and prayer work. After all this prep work was complete, I "let go and let God." Spirit then provided the grace that brought me the desired result without any further effort on my part. And last but not least, I kept my heart open to receive, knowing I would be blessed with a divine answer. This simple process produced miraculous results.

Gifts From Gregory

Looking for the gifts in Gregory's short life has been very healing for me. My mom taught me that we could always look back and see the good in any situation no matter how bad the circumstances. However, with Gregory's death, I could not see any benefit in the early years. I kept asking, "Why did he have to leave?"

Since my spiritual awakening, I've shifted my view of this event and have therefore been able to identify quite a few benefits. The most wonderful blessing from Gregory is the joy of our spirit connection. Feeling his spiritual presence is such a gift! It has totally changed who I am and how I see the world.

Another important gift is the many ways I have grown and changed as an individual. I took the step-by-step journey of choices that led me to loving and honoring myself, and then sent that love flowing out into the world.

My experience with Gregory has also given me great empathy for other mothers who have lost a child. My healing journey actually prepared me for a role I never dreamed would be asked of me—assisting my own daughter, Coreen, when her first baby died during labor and delivery. From personal experience, I could understand her doubts, her guilt-ridden, fearful thoughts, and her heartache. It became my mission to provide my daughter with the opportunity to talk about her grief and any other feelings she needed to express. I was able to support Coreen during this tragic time, because I had already cleared my emotional baggage and come to forgiveness about my own loss. I could feel my spirit son right beside me, inspiring me as I comforted and cared for my daughter. I know deep in my heart, that Ethan, Coreen's dear baby, is with Gregory on the other side.

The greatest blessing from Gregory has been my own healing. Through our connection, I have healed on many levels! I've also become an ordained minister and a certified practitioner of Radiant Heart Healing. Both programs gave me the skills to use energy work for deep self-healing. I know I will continue to use meditation, prayers, and journaling to keep a strong connection with my spirit son. It's become a way of life that feeds my soul.

My healing journey has been the best thing that ever happened to me. I now see both my cancer and my experience with Gregory as blessings in disguise. I have awakened to Spirit, and my life is filled with a "joy of being" as I move forward on my earthly soul journey.

Four Years Later

After healing on many levels and enjoying four years of good health, I've lost my remission. I was shocked and saddened to be dealing with cancer again—indeed, I felt like my body betrayed me. This news was such a blow! It's still a complete mystery as to why it happened.

I decided to follow the doctors' recommendations to do chemo, radiation, and a stem cell transplant. At the same time, I deepened my prayer work and my meditation practices. Within days, I was able to gather courage from Gregory and all the spiritual beings he brought into my life. Mother Mary became my constant companion with her blue energy surrounding me like a protective cloak. I thanked my spirit son every day for opening the door to this blessed connection.

Visions of Gregory

During this time of increased need, Gregory was there for me. Previously, over the ten years of our contact, I felt his energy in my hands, sensed his presence in the room, heard his voice, or let his words come into my mind. Yet, all this time, I never had a vision of my son.

Then one day while lying in bed recovering from chemo, I had an unforgettable experience. I called Gregory's name and within seconds, his energy enveloped me in an embrace. It was so magnificent to be wrapped in his love! As the hug ended, I saw Gregory in my mind's eye. What a breathtaking surprise! Never in my wildest dreams did I expect to receive such a gift! This first vision of my spirit son will remain in my heart forever.

Gregory appeared as a young man—slender, but strong—with dark hair. He seemed to be about twenty years old. We talked a bit, and I gave him this message of gratitude, "Thank you for all the gifts you have given me over the years. You started my journey on this healing path when you opened the door to the other side, so I could connect with Mother Mary, my angels, and my other guides. You are still my connection to the spirit world."

On my birthday, I called Gregory's name and he showed up again as an attractive young man. In this vision, we looked deeply into each other's eyes as we stood facing one another with our hands held up palm-to-palm. I felt the love energy flow through me. It was such pure love! I wept with the joy of it. All I could say was, "Thank you, God. Thank you, Gregory. Thank you for the awesome birthday present!"

Weeks later, when I called his name during meditation, Gregory appeared again as a tall, handsome young man. First, he hugged me. Then he took my hand and gracefully held it high as he began to twirl me around. We looked like beautiful figurines on a music box. And we danced! It was so exquisite! The vision was so beautiful it took my breath away! Tears of joy flowed down my face as my heart filled with love and gratitude for this extraordinary gift.

A Phone Conversation With Dr. Wesch

I lost my remission eighteen months ago, and I'm deeply saddened that the cancer has progressed with a vengeance. My doctors tell me there are no more medical options available. So now it's time for me to focus my attention on creating a peaceful dying process.

Now everything revolves around my quality of life. I'm fighting for my emotional needs as wells as for my physical needs—like staying out of pain. I'm talking with my family and sharing my beliefs about dying peacefully. This feels so right. Words of wisdom just come out of my mouth, and it's such a wonderful feeling to be so clear. I feel Spirit bringing these words to me; I know I'm channeling because I have such clarity about all this. I'm teaching my whole soul group that one's quality of life is the most important thing! And I know it's part of my soul purpose to do this.

I've been studying consciousness for fifteen years without knowing why. Now I know it was to prepare for this moment in time when I'm to be the teacher about a person's quality of life at the end of the earthly journey. I'm also teaching my family and others about what it's like to die with dignity. I know deep within my heart this is an important facet of my soul purpose. Finally, I know what I've been preparing for all this time.

Mother Mary is my constant companion now—she's always by my side. During one of her visits she held my hand and said, "Blessed daughter, when the time comes I will take your hand and make the journey with you to the other side. Have no fear. You will not be alone." And so I am at peace.

I also know my beloved Gregory, will be there to welcome me Home because, as he told me, our souls are connected for all time.

Mary's Transition

Several weeks after I had this phone conversation with Mary, she made a very peaceful transition at home surrounded by her beloved family. Her husband and family sent out this announcement: "Mary rose to a higher level on Friday, June 6th." Indeed, she did!

Points to Ponder

Mary's healing journey has a very dramatic beginning—a diagnosis of cancer. She begins using meditation and prayer to gain some insight about the spiritual aspects of her illness, never thinking, for even a moment, that she might connect with the soul of Gregory, her beloved baby who died twenty-five years earlier. In this touching story, we are blessed to witness Mary's feelings of wonder and absolute joy as she slowly awakens to knowing she is—and always has been—receiving guidance and inspiration from her spirit son. This is a huge shift in consciousness! And after this awakening, Mary does not go back to sleep.

Mary tells us it is Gregory who opened the door to the spirit world. This opening allows Mary to receive healing from the angels and many ascended masters, including her namesake, Mother Mary, who is often called "the mother of all mothers." At the end of her earthly journey, we see this dedicated spiritual seeker approaching her own death with absolutely no fear, having the reassurance from Mother Mary, "I will take your hand and make the journey with you to the other side." She is also able to fulfill her soul purpose of teaching others about dying with dignity.

You might be wondering why Mary's cancer returned after she had accomplished so much healing and resolved so many emotional issues. There's no clear answer to this question. It's one of those mysteries of life that we are not privy to understand. However, it's important to remember that spiritual healing is not about the survival of the physical body; *it's about the completion of the soul's purpose.* Before crossing to the other side, Mary completed the spiritual lessons of her son's death—she achieved a state of grace and forgiveness, and was able to shift her perspective so she could find the gifts in the tragedy of infant loss. As in the Inca tradition, Gregory brought powerful medicine to his mother so she could heal at the soul level.

This story is an amazing testimony to the many benefits of seeking deep spiritual healing after infant death. Mary uses her experiences with her spirit son to transform herself and evolve to higher levels of consciousness for the remaining years of her life here on earth. Perhaps even more importantly, she also transforms the quality of her death.

Did it ever occur to you that, like Mary and Gregory, you and your beloved baby are connected for all time? Gregory tells us this is true whether you know it or not. Can you imagine your baby as a powerful soul who sends you inspiration and guidance each night while you sleep? And furthermore, can you also embrace the idea that this ageless soul you call "baby" is a magnificent, loving being who will greet you at the gates of heaven when it's your time to go Home? Your fear of death might just dissipate as you allow these teachings from Gregory to become part of your beliefs about the afterlife.

My heart is filled with a deep spiritual peace as I imagine this sweet, loving soul we call Mary connecting once again with her spirit son in heaven. If you listen with your heart, you might hear her saying, *"Gregory was there to meet me as I entered the gates of heaven. And we danced!"*

Chapter Five

The Joy of Sacred Work

Molly came as a powerful partner rather than a little baby needing care.
She is very much alive and has been supporting me
in the soul work that I came here to do.
—Maureen, Molly's Mother

Reverend Maureen is a most unusual person—she is an ordained minister, a hospital chaplain, a Reiki Master, and a spiritual healer. She presents herself as any one of these depending on the need of the moment. When we first met, she talked about her various roles and said with a quiet laugh, "Only in California! It's more open here, you know."

Maureen's story, like all the others in this book, came to me without any effort on my part. Our introduction was clearly not an accident. Indeed, it was another one of those synchronistic meetings, like Wachan, the Inca medicine man appearing on my path in Sedona. Spirit wanted this story in this book. And so it is!

Connecting With Maureen

My first connection with Maureen was a voice on the phone. After a professional colleague told her about Radiant Heart Healing, she called from California to inquire about my work. Her passion for life was quite obvious, and immediately, I could feel her wonderful, high frequency energy. We agreed she would come for a private, three-day retreat at my home in the Indiana Dunes. While on the phone, I had no clue about Maureen's history, but I had a feeling the weekend would be quite special. I was not disappointed!

As we began our work together, this openhearted woman shared her life story with me. For the previous twenty-five years, she had been on a fascinating journey of spiritual transformation, and the catalyst for her evolution was the death of her beloved infant. When I heard this, I knew why Spirit brought us together.

Maureen's Life Story

Maureen, age twenty-three, and her husband, Tom, were happily married and living in a suburb of San Francisco. Parents of a one-year-old daughter, they were looking forward to the birth of their second child. Their ordinary life was unfolding exactly as they had planned: Tom had a secure job, Maureen was home full-time with the baby, and another bundle of joy was about to arrive. Then fate intervened with the swiftness of lightning, and life was never the same for Maureen or Tom.

There was some confusion about the due date for this second child, so the doctors told Maureen it was a good idea to induce labor. She agreed and delivered a beautiful baby girl named Molly.

Intuitively, Maureen knew there was a serious problem the very moment Molly was born. She started screaming, "There's something wrong with my baby. Help her! Help her!" The doctors assured her the baby was fine, but they rushed Molly to another room and gave Maureen a sedative to calm her down. She was not allowed to hold her baby girl or even to see her.

Two hours later, Maureen's husband came into her room and said, "Molly is very sick. Her lungs are not developed enough, and she's having trouble breathing. The doctors are working with her down in the nursery." With that, one of the doctors gave Maureen a strong tranquilizer, and she slipped into a deep sleep. A few hours later, Maureen woke up with a start and went to see Molly in the nursery. Molly wasn't there. When Maureen couldn't find her daughter, she began screaming hysterically. The nurses finally told her that her baby had been transferred to another hospital that had special equipment to help Molly's breathing. After two days of struggling to breathe, Molly died. Tom went to the other hospital and saw Molly after she died, but no one thought to include Maureen.

The policy at the hospital, as was common at that time, was to whisk the infant away and bury the body in an unmarked grave. Maureen was never allowed to hold—or even see—her little girl. The family held a memorial for Molly, but there was no casket and no burial as part of the service. Although Maureen attended this ceremony, she was in such a state that she has only vague memories of being there.

Denying Molly's Existence

Maureen did not seek professional counseling for her devastating grief because it just didn't occur to her. She listened to her father, who told her, "It's over. Stop crying and don't ever think about it again." He also established an unwritten rule for the entire extended family: "Don't ever mention Molly's name." The minute the wake was over, no one in the family spoke of Molly again. Maureen went on with her life as if nothing had ever happened, and there was no acknowledgment of her grief. Even her husband wasn't willing to talk about the death of their baby. Everyone acted as if Molly had never existed.

Maureen became pregnant three months later and had a miscarriage. Again, there was no recognition or discussion of Maureen's grief. Two months later, she happily became pregnant again, but during the entire nine months, she had nightmares about this baby dying. Thankfully, the pregnancy was uneventful, and she was gifted with a healthy baby girl.

Beginning the Healing Journey

Maureen thought she was doing something good for herself by denying her grief and following her father's decree not to talk about Molly. Maureen described how she created various coping mechanisms to keep her grief suppressed.

> *I held it together during those years by overworking and always being very busy. I fought a serious depression by always being active. Fourteen years after Molly's death, I started to weep for no apparent reason. I had these uncontrollable crying jags that just came on out of the blue. It never dawned on me that my tears had anything to do with Molly's death.*

After a year of crying episodes, Maureen "accidentally" stumbled into a situation where she received some assistance with her emotional pain. She felt inspired to become a minister in the Episcopal Church. This decision was quite surprising to Maureen—she had never before had the desire to go in that direction. At the time, this courageous woman didn't have a clue why she made this decision. She just knew she had to do it.

The first part of her ministerial training included a two-week retreat focused on emotions and helping people deal with grief issues. For the first time in fifteen years, Maureen heard that it was normal and natural to grieve the death of her infant daughter. She spent hours and hours talking about her hospital experiences when Molly died. Maureen relived the heart-wrenching days of Molly's birth and death, pouring out her feelings to a compassionate counselor who supported her in releasing all the repressed grief, anger, and guilt. Maureen's wounded heart began to heal.

A Dream Visitation

Two weeks after that ministerial retreat, Maureen woke one morning with the memory of a dream about Molly. This was the first time Maureen was aware of any spirit contact with her baby girl. She reported it with so much joy.

In the dream, I have an appointment, but I don't know what it's about. I ask my husband to go with me, but he says no. Then I ask my parents to go, and they say no too. So I think to myself, "Well, then I'll just go by myself." I walk into a house and find myself in a very large room filled with all these joyful people who greet me by name. They are very happy to see me. Then there seems to be a great parting—like the parting of the Red Sea. I'm led through a chasm of people into another room.

There I see a little girl about seven or eight years old. She's sitting on a church altar, and she's surrounded by many beings. She's beautiful! "Radiant" is the best word to describe her. I also see this magnificent light surrounding her. As I go up to her, she looks at me and says, "Mommy! Mommy!" I know immediately, without question, that it's Molly. I call out her name, "Molly! Molly!" She looks at me and says, "Mommy, I'm okay. I'm safe."

Then I'm led up to Molly. I kneel in front of her and put my head in her lap. She strokes my hair so gently it feels like angel wings touching me. She keeps saying over and over again, "I'm okay. I'm okay." She continues caressing my hair for a very long time, and I feel her loving me with every stroke. The love coming from her is so incredible!

I desperately needed to hear Molly say she was okay. I had always worried about her. I had never held her, and I didn't even know where she was buried. I often wondered where she was in the spirit world. I didn't know where she was in body or spirit. In this dream, my spirit baby was reassuring me and telling me that I didn't have to worry anymore. It was the exact message I needed. Molly's visit was such a gift!

I had such guilt after her death because I believed I was not a good mother. Molly was born before her little lungs were able to function. In hindsight, we realized she needed more time in the womb. I felt her death was my fault because I allowed the doctor to induce labor.

I didn't really understand there was any hint of danger in this decision when I agreed to it. In those days, people trusted their doctors and didn't question their instructions. I never thought I had a choice. My guilt simply vanished after Molly came in the dream.

Here we see Molly's messages of deep love and reassurance resolving years of guilt and fear in just a few sacred moments. The healing flowed in like grace with little effort on Maureen's part. This is the power of Spirit! Like the Inca spirit babies, Molly sent her grieving mother potent medicine.

You may be wondering why there was no communication between Maureen and her beloved spirit baby for fifteen years. I believe Maureen's blocked grief created a dam that prevented the flow of spiritual energies between this mother and her daughter in heaven. Maureen's release work at the retreat broke that dam, and thus allowed the floodwaters of spirit communication to flow from heaven down to earth. Only then could the healing journey begin.

After this dream experience, Maureen was free to tell her story. She broke her father's rule and began talking about Molly, her intense grief, releasing her pain at the retreat, and the gift of Molly coming in her dream. At first, she cried whenever she told her story; then, gradually, the tears stopped, and she could share her story with compassion and love.

Finding Soul Purpose

Three years after the dream experience (eighteen years after Molly's death), Rev. Maureen began working as a hospital chaplain and was privileged to minister to other parents who had just lost their babies. She described her experience those first days on duty at the hospital.

I knew exactly what to say. The words of compassion flowed easily, and I was able to touch the hearts of these grieving mothers and fathers. I told them my story when it seemed appropriate. Sometimes I even told them my dream about Molly. It seemed to bring some relief to their terrible grief and a bit of hope that their baby was also safe somewhere in the spirit world beyond where we can see, hear, and touch.

Rev. Maureen loved her role as chaplain in the hospital. Dealing with one crisis after another was very demanding work, yet she seemed to blossom. She carried out her tasks with great passion and always had the energy to rise to the occasion and be there to comfort another set of parents when they heard the terrible news, "Your baby is not going to make it." At the end of most days, Rev. Maureen felt tired yet fulfilled. She often said to herself, "This is the work I came here to do."

The doctors in the hospital knew Rev. Maureen was comfortable dealing with death, and they relied on her whenever a baby or young child was dying. Some doctors even came to talk to her about their own feelings after the death of an infant.

Soon after starting her work as a chaplain, this woman with an inquisitive spirit was guided to train in Reiki, a Japanese form of healing introduced in the United States during the early eighties. Rev. Maureen loved learning to be a channel for this spiritual energy and gradually began integrating it into her chaplain's work at the hospital. She found it to be a wonderful way to help anxious parents shift into a state of spiritual peace. Although sixty percent of hospitals now offer Reiki to their patients, this was not always so; Reverend Maureen was one of the pioneers in this movement.

A Joyful, Powerful Partner

After Maureen shared her life story, we began the first healing session of her retreat. As we sat together in my meditation room, neither Maureen nor I had any idea where Spirit would lead us. Together, we said a prayer inviting support and inspiration from our angels, our spirit guides, and Molly. Surprisingly, we were guided to release some of Maureen's unresolved early childhood pain. As we finished this clearing process, I instructed Maureen to fill her heart with the healing energy of divine love using the Radiant Heart Healing visualization:

- Use your imagination to open a spot on the top of your head.
- Send an imaginary funnel out into the universe.
- Connect with an unlimited ball of radiant healing energy—it's a bright light.
- Bring that light through your head, neck, and shoulders.
- Fill your heart with this light, which is actually divine love.

I sat on the couch beside Maureen doing the same visualization, so I could fill my own heart with divine love and send it through my hands into her heart. As we proceeded, I could feel both of us moving into a very sacred space. I began thinking about Mother Mary, so I assumed she was present and assisting us. There also seemed to be another spirit right in front of us, and I felt this being sending another shaft of light into Maureen's heart. I asked Maureen if she was sensing anything in the spirit world; her answer confirmed everything I was getting intuitively. Here is Maureen's description of her experience.

I see a ray of soft, pink light come into my heart from the front. Then Molly's face emerges from the mist in front of me. She looks a lot like me, and she has my oldest daughter's nose. She is sending the pink energy of unconditional love. There is so much love!

She's sending me lots of messages, too. She's saying I need to play more and that I can always come and play with her. I see her spirit with my spirit and Mother Mary dancing in the light. We are playing ring-around-the-rosy. We are all laughing so joyfully. What fun!

She's telling me she is very proud of me as a mother. She died so I could know how to work with grieving parents. She was very glad to do this. It was this wonderful thing she could do for me. She isn't sad or grieving about it. She is so joyful as she talks to me about it. She has her hands on my face, giving me this very gentle caress.

This second appearance of Molly brought another level of healing. Molly came as a powerful partner rather than a little baby needing care. She is very much alive and has been supporting me in the soul work that I came here to do. She's just like my other two daughters, who are alive here on earth with me. All three of them are my partners, and they love me unconditionally. Molly's "just one of the girls."

I knew since the first dream that my grief experience with Molly's birth and death prepared me for my work with grieving parents. However, this communication from Molly allowed me to see the joy she had in carrying out her part of the plan. Feeling the absolute joy flowing from Molly is a gift I will always treasure.

When Molly came to me in that dream, she freed me from my guilt and gave me my freedom. She also gave me the wisdom to do this work with other grieving parents.

I finally understand that Molly's birth and death are both part of a bigger plan, so I can fulfill my soul purpose and do the work I came here to do. Without this experience, I would never have known the depth of these grieving parents' heartache. I am forever thankful for Molly and all we have shared together. It's taken me twenty-five years to get it. I now understand.

This moment of clarity about the purpose of Molly's birth and death came unbidden—it truly flowed into Maureen's consciousness on the wings of grace, and brought a deeper meaning to the tragedy of her baby's death. And as she received this clarity, Maureen spontaneously experienced another level of healing. In addition, witnessing her daughter's great delight transformed Maureen's last bits of unhealed grief into joy. She now consistently thinks of her spirit baby with love instead of pain. This is the very definition of transformational healing.

Twenty-five years seems like a long time when we view Maureen's healing journey with our human eyes. However, because her transformation took place at the soul level—not the personality level—we must look at her spiritual path with our soul eyes. Our common measurements of time—hours, days, months, and years—do not even exist at the soul level. Indeed, soul time stretches into eternity as opposed to years on the human calendar. So from the perspective of soul time, Maureen's journey of evolution happened in the blink of an eye.

Observing the Soul Light

Ten years after our weekend retreat, Rev. Maureen and I met for lunch while I was traveling and teaching in California. Knowing Maureen's life was Spirit-guided, I was excited to hear how her journey had unfolded since we had last met.

During that time, Rev. Maureen continued her soul mission of integrating Reiki with her counseling as a hospital chaplain. She also began to investigate many different avenues for personal and professional growth. This intuitive woman followed her heart and was led to explore more and more in the area of mind-body medicine and spiritual healing. Rev. Maureen traveled all over the country taking extensive experiential training programs with leaders in a fast-growing field called energy medicine, or soul medicine.

Maureen's ability to sense the higher frequency energies of the spirit world increased as she raised her own level of vibration in these training programs. She came to know that Molly was always present, guiding and inspiring her work with families who were grieving after the death of a beloved infant. Eventually, Maureen developed the gift of spiritual sight—she became clairvoyant! This gift often develops when anyone spends a great deal of time in meditation. Rev. Maureen said, "I don't have time to sit and meditate with my eyes closed every day. However, I'm in a constant state of meditation as I do my work at the hospital. I simply let Spirit flow through me. It's the only way to do this work!"

As Rev. Maureen made her rounds in the hospital, she often tuned in to the interpenetrating spirit world and saw a bubble of divine light around the babies and children as they lay in their hospital beds. When a child was dying, angels appeared and surrounded the family members gathered at the scene. Using her clairvoyant abilities, Rev. Maureen sometimes even saw the spirit of a baby leave this world and slip into the heavenly realm.

I had the gift of "being with" a mother named Sara as her beloved son was dying in the NICU. Sara knew these were to be her very last minutes on earth with her baby. She cradled him in the crook of her arm, and gazing with love at her son, gently crooned to him that it was okay to go.

As I was silently praying and holding sacred space for this mother and son, time slowed down and the veil between the two worlds disappeared, allowing me to see both dimensions simultaneously. I watched in fascination as this scene unfolded.

A shaft of light came down through the ceiling in front of the mother and went directly into the baby's heart. It was composed of luminescent white light—like mother-of-pearl—and was about six inches in diameter. Next, a cone of purple energy came out of the mother's forehead (third eye) and connected with the shaft of light at the baby's heart. Then the soul energy began to lift out of the baby's heart, wafting and swirling like smoke as it traveled up through the glimmering shaft of light.

I was awe struck! I knew without question I was being given the gift of observing the baby's soul as it started the journey Home.

I wanted confirmation and support for my interpretation of this profound experience, so I called my spiritual mentor and described what I had witnessed. She responded, "Yes, you were observing the baby's soul leaving his body, and the mother's soul was helping the child to make the transition—that's what that purple light was all about." This information about the purple light was such a blessing.

Months later, Rev. Maureen was called to another deathbed scene as parents took their precious infant off life support. Each end-of-life experience is as unique as the people involved. In this case, the mother had come to acceptance and was lovingly holding their dying son; in contrast, the baby's father was still very much struggling with the idea of saying his final goodbyes.

When an infant is dying, Rev. Maureen stays in the background and intervenes at the human level only when invited into the family circle. She was sitting quietly sending divine love energy to give spiritual support to this precious infant and both parents when her soul vision spontaneously opened.

> *First, I observed an energetic, cobalt blue grid across the front of the mother; the baby also had the same cobalt grid, and it was interpenetrating with the mother's. These grids were so apparent—I couldn't miss that electric blue color. In my healing classes, I learned about the matrix that surrounds each human being; I'd seen pictures of it, but had never seen it with my own eyes.*

> *Next, a luminescent mother-of-pearl cylinder of light came down over the baby and expanded to encompass both parents. The essence of the baby left his body in a stream of bright light, flowed over to touch the father, and then continued up the cylinder through the ceiling. As this was happening, I intuitively understood that the baby's soul went over to comfort the father before leaving. I knew I had just witnessed the miracle of love.*

The eternal soul of this infant obviously had intention, intelligence, and great compassion for his grieving father. Very few people have Rev. Maureen's gift of spiritual sight. Consequently, most people who witness the death of an infant are unaware that something wonderful and very loving is taking place at the soul level when a baby goes Home. Though many feel abandoned by God when their precious baby dies, Maureen's visions remind us that God is ever-present and providing the miracle of love in those holy moments. Maureen's visions also remind us of the Inca cultural beliefs: when a beloved baby transitions to the other side, the spirit of that baby brings healing to the grieving family members.

Points to Ponder

Maureen uses a terrible tragedy—her baby's death—as the crucible for her own joyous, spiritual transformation. Over a period of eighteen years, she transforms herself from a severely depressed, grieving wife and mother to a dedicated hospital chaplain who is passionate about counseling families after the death of a beloved infant or child. This work feeds her soul. It is her calling, her mission, her soul purpose!

Our life here on earth is meant to be a continuous process of seeking, learning, growing, expanding, and raising our vibration higher and higher until we master the lessons we came to learn, complete our soul purpose, and then return Home. Spiritual seekers ask questions like, *"Who am I? Why am I here? What spiritual lessons am I here to learn?"* Maureen shows us that it is sometimes a long, slow journey to discover the answers to these universal questions.

Like Molly, your spirit baby is also a powerful partner with the ability to support you in your soul work. Have you answered these important questions for yourself? *Why am I here? What am I to do? What lessons am I to learn?* It's an exciting journey to discover your own unique answers. And remember, you are not alone as you search. Your spirit baby is calling: *"Come this way. This work will light up your life. I'm here to support you as you follow your joy."*

CHAPTER SIX

Soul Agreements

*I got the message that we had all agreed
to this before we ever came here.
I just have to trust that we all accomplished
our prearranged intentions.*
—*Sandy, Melissa's Mother*

Mike and Sandy are very grounded Midwesterners who have created a unique home in the rolling farmlands of Ohio. They've spent the last thirty years working side by side for endless hours as they renovated an old barn that dates back to the 1800s. Their beautiful home is filled with polished antiques, several brick fireplaces, and an abundance of love. The energy of peace and love envelops everyone who walks through the door.

Mike is now seventy-five years old, but says he feels more like forty-five. He retired in his mid-fifties following heart surgery that involved five bypass procedures. Before his retirement, Mike worked for thirty-five years as a civilian war logistics planner for the Department of the Air Force. As a self-taught carpenter, plumber, and electrician, Mike completed the majority of the remodeling work on the old barn.

Sandy is a nurse as well as a great cook. She loves to feed large groups of friends and family in her big country kitchen, which is decked out with a red checked gingham tablecloth and curtains to match. Their three grown children return home often with their spouses and the grandchildren to enjoy Sandy's cooking and the wonderful, loving atmosphere.

Sandy's love for her ten grandchildren is evident everywhere you look—pictures on the refrigerator, the antique high chair in the corner, and a sign that says:

*Nana's Kitchen—Open 24 Hours
Where memories are made
and grandkids are spoiled.*

Mike and Sandy are two of the most down-to-earth people you could ever meet, but when you look a little deeper, you'll find two of the most spiritual people walking on the planet. They both attribute their spiritual awakening to the birth and death of their third child, Melissa, who was born almost forty years ago, and only lived seven months. Melissa never came home from the hospital to this beautiful place in the woods, but she transformed the whole family without ever speaking a word.

Sandy's God Experience

Sandy's pregnancy with Melissa was without complications, and the labor and delivery were extremely fast. In fact, Melissa came so quickly, she had to be delivered by the nurses who were moving Sandy through the hospital hallways on a gurney. Sandy described her unforgettable mystical experience when Melissa was born.

> *I was feeling the urge to push as I arrived at the hospital, and Melissa came before we could get to the delivery room. I know I left my body while Melissa was being born. I remember being up in the right-hand corner of the ceiling looking down. There was a man reading a newspaper in the hallway, and I could look down on his paper as he held it in front of him. This happened to me before I'd ever heard of an out-of-body experience.*

> *There just aren't words to describe the feeling that came over me. All I can tell you is that I felt a Oneness—God and I were one. It was the most wonderful peace and love I've ever felt. It was so wonderful that I was more excited about this experience than Melissa's birth.*

> *I remember when Mike came in to see us; he was all excited about our baby. I kept trying to talk about my God experience. I was saying, "Something happened to me. I have to tell you about this." He ignored everything I was saying and kept his focus on Melissa.*

Sandy was extremely disappointed in Mike's reaction. Right then and there, she decided to keep quiet about her mystical experience. She felt that if Mike didn't believe her, probably no one else would either. However, she kept trying to make sense of what had happened. She even asked the nurses if she was given any drugs that would induce hallucinations. They assured her there had been no time to give her any medications. By the end of the day, Sandy denied her exquisite spiritual encounter.

> *My spiritual experience was wonderful. It was not scary at all. However, I pushed it away because it just didn't fit into anything I knew. I even used to think, "Maybe it didn't even happen." It wasn't until years later that I understood what this was all about.*

Something Is Terribly Wrong

Within the first twenty-four hours, Sandy knew something was terribly wrong with Melissa when she did not want to nurse and seemed rather detached. The first few days Melissa kept losing weight, so the doctors did some extensive testing and found she had a bowel blockage and a severe infection throughout her digestive system. Melissa was actually starving to death. The doctors had to remove most of her intestines to save her life.

The months following this first surgery were a roller coaster for Mike, Sandy, and their precious baby girl. Melissa had seven bowel surgeries over a period of seven months. After each surgery, adhesions would form another bowel blockage. It was a catch-22 situation. Melissa couldn't live with the adhesions, but each time the doctors operated to remove them, the procedure caused even more. Sandy remembers being very angry with the surgeon. Every time she saw him walking towards, her she knew it was more bad news, so she hated seeing him come.

After the seventh surgery, the surgeon came out and said Melissa's intestines were growing. They had grown seven inches! This indeed was a miracle! At last, a ray of hope! The doctors even said that Melissa had improved so much she could leave the hospital in a few days. Mike and Sandy were jubilant, absolutely thrilled to be taking their precious baby girl home at last.

Sadly, their joy lasted less than twenty-four hours. The next morning the nurse called and said, "Come to the hospital right away. Melissa is dying."

During the night, Melissa had developed a massive infection that swept through her entire body, and there was nothing the doctors could do. Sandy and Mike kept an all-night vigil before Melissa finally passed. During the night, Sandy finally came to terms with Melissa's death and made the decision to let her go.

> *I felt this incredible sense of peace and love come over me. It was the exact same feeling I had during the God experience when Melissa was born. At that point, I was able to let her go. Up until then, I just knew she wasn't going to die—that's all there was to it. Melissa died within eight hours of my releasing her.*

Love Is Supposed to Protect Your Kids

Sandy was very disturbed by her feelings of helplessness in the face of this tragedy with Melissa.

What bothered me the most was that I felt like a failure. When you're a mother, your love is supposed to protect your kids; yet, I couldn't protect this baby. I remember when they moved Melissa out of intensive care to a regular floor. I went to the hospital more often and stayed longer. I was thinking, "I'll get you well. My love will get you well." And then I couldn't do it. I kept wondering what was wrong that I couldn't do it.

Mike had no expectation that he could protect Melissa with his love. He bonded with his daughter when she was first born, but was able to let go and accept the possibility of Melissa's death much sooner than Sandy.

When she was born, we were told about all the medical problems she was going through. It was devastating to hear this news. Melissa had her third operation when she was about three months old. I just got a gut feeling that she wasn't meant to be with us. I tried sharing this feeling with Sandy, but there was no way she would accept this idea.

I bonded with the baby in the beginning, but then I released her after that third surgery. Sandy kept trying to change my mind. She would sort of force the bonding issue by asking me to hold Melissa. That's the only time I would hold her. I just didn't want to feel that bond again.

The "Why" Questions

While Melissa was struggling to live, Mike started building some resentment towards God.

We would look at Melissa, and we could see pain in her little eyes. That just tore us up. I remember asking, "God, why is this happening? Why does this little baby have to go through this? Why would You let an innocent baby suffer like this? Why don't You just take her? Why do we all have to go through this? You're just going to take this baby away from us anyway. Please take her now."

Sandy was just the opposite, so I never shared any of these thoughts with her. It used to break my heart when I'd see my wife holding Melissa at the hospital. I could sense the pain that Sandy was feeling and that would just tear me up even more.

I kept asking all these questions, but I just couldn't get any answers. It was like a nightmare. I tried to find a reason that made sense to me, but I never did reach that point. I never did get any feeling about it.

Another thing that got to me was how unfair it was to our other children; Michael was just six years old, and Maryann was only sixteen months. We were spending four hours a day at the hospital while our children at home needed us. I was very upset that they were staying with neighbors all the time.

Mike plunged into the depths of despair when he couldn't get any answers to his questions. He felt abandoned by God, and this wounded him to the very core. Without answers there was nothing to do but continue to function at his daily routines—going to work, doing his chores around the house, parenting their other two children, and visiting Melissa at the hospital. He went through the motions, but his heart just wasn't in it. His spirit was broken by the deep grief that he tried to suppress.

Sandy didn't start asking the "why" questions until after Melissa's death. At the funeral, a friend said to Sandy, "Melissa suffered for your sins." This statement ignited Sandy's anger, and she told the friend, "I don't believe that for a minute."

During our interview, Sandy said:

That statement made me mad! But then I started wondering if that was possible. That's when I started asking the "why" questions. Could God ask a baby to suffer for my sins? I decided I didn't have much use for a God who would let a baby suffer like that. I couldn't accept any of it.

Buried Grief and New Joy

Mike and Sandy simply could not deal with their grief after Melissa's death. Sandy stated, "I couldn't even talk about Melissa for the first few years." Instead, she threw herself into the roles of homemaker and mother, and joined every organization she could find. Mike also kept himself very busy as a way to bury his grief about their baby girl. At the time, they didn't know what else to do.

Sandy soon discovered she was pregnant again—this baby was due approximately two years after Melissa's birth. Mike and Sandy were both elated about this news because they had always intended to have a big family. They also wanted to move on with their lives, so focusing their attention on this new baby allowed both of them to push their painful memories about Melissa even further into the background.

Naturally, both Mike and Sandy had many fears during the pregnancy and were very much on edge the entire time. As was their way, they both kept a stiff upper lip and didn't even talk to each other about their apprehensions. It was a very stressful nine months—being worried, yet pretending not to be.

Sandy delivered a healthy baby girl. What a blessing! Both parents and the whole extended family were able to relax once they brought her home from the hospital. Mike and Sandy named her Kelly, and everyone focused on the joy and excitement of loving this new, little addition to the family. Her birth was such a gift.

Finding Purpose—A Gift From Melissa

Four years after Melissa's death, when Kelly was two years old, Sandy enrolled in nursing school to become a hospice nurse. She was running very hard to avoid her buried grief, and she made sure she didn't have time to think or feel. She even started a catering business doing wedding cakes to pay for her school tuition. Sandy was overwhelmed the entire time, and she wanted it that way.

She described her strong motivation to stay in nursing school during this difficult stage of her life.

> *The gift I got from Melissa's death was the motivation to become a hospice nurse. It was a passion I couldn't deny, a gift I will treasure my whole life.*

> *I was in a terrible state after Melissa's death, but I also felt this inner urge to do something so other parents wouldn't have to go through what we did.*

> *I decided I had to make sense of the death of our baby. My way of doing this was to go back to school to become a hospice nurse. I made that decision in the hospital when I was watching the nurses take care of our infant. I wouldn't call it cold—maybe "clinical" is a good word for it.*

> *Mike and I always felt we were intruding when we visited Melissa. We would stand by the window of the nursery praying they would let us in. Sometimes they did, but often they didn't. It seemed to be a bother to the staff that we were there. Of course, forty years ago nobody in healthcare thought about the emotional needs of a family with a dying baby.*

> *Melissa died painfully in the hospital. I saw her struggle as the nurses forced air into her lungs. It was hard to see her being forced to hold on when she was exhausted and ready to go. Finally her*

heart stopped, and they wanted to shock her with the paddles to get her heart started again. I refused. I held her and she died in my arms.

I just kept thinking, "There has to be a better way." This thought kept me motivated. I wanted to become a hospice nurse so I could help others die with peace and dignity.

Many times Sandy thought of dropping out of school because they had no money to pay the tuition for the upcoming semester. Then the phone would ring, and someone would order a wedding cake. They would write Sandy a check, and it would be the exact amount needed to pay the fees for the next semester. At the time, Sandy was very grateful that she could continue her education, but she didn't see the bigger picture. She was not aware that all of these blessings were synchronistic gifts guided by Spirit.

At this point, Mike was also unaware that Spirit was guiding him. He continued working at the military base, being an active parent to their three children, working on remodeling the old barn, and denying his grief about Melissa. He simply did not want to talk about Melissa or do anything active about working through his grief.

In his mid-fifties, Mike retired from his position as a war planner for the Air Force, and he and Sandy opened an antiques business in their home. Sandy was still attending nursing school part time, yet she decided to join her husband in this new venture. They both loved people as well as antiques, so working together in the business energized and uplifted them. Indeed, Sandy had even more energy to devote to her studies.

Because Sandy could attend nursing school only part time, it was very slow going. Finally, twelve years after Melissa's death, she accomplished her goal of becoming a hospice nurse. She described some of the benefits she received from this work.

I loved being with dying patients—I loved my connection to them. I was trained to encourage family and friends to be with the dying patient, the opposite of my experience with Melissa. It was the most satisfying work I've ever done. If I hadn't worked at hospice, I would have had a much harder time accepting a lot of this spiritual stuff.

We had nurses who could tell us when death was going to occur because they could see angels around the patient. They always knew. We just came to accept it; after a while, it became so normal that it wasn't a big deal. Nothing surprised us anymore.

From my very first days, hospice patients were describing out-of-body experiences, near-death experiences, seeing angels and deceased loved ones, and seeing the light. It became kind of routine because so many different patients were telling me their unique experiences—yet they all had the linking thread of seeing light and spiritual beings in the world beyond.

From listening to the descriptions of these dying patients, I began to understand my own out-of-body experience when Melissa was born. I stopped denying the truth of what happened that day. I finally realized it was a profound spiritual moment! Now I understand it was God saying to me, "It's going to be okay. This is okay, so just remember that."

In retrospect, all of these reports of spiritual experiences from patients and staff at hospice prepared me for what was to take place in the future as I moved forward, healing my grief.

Of course, all this time Sandy did not have a clue that her life was unfolding in accordance with the calling of her soul. She was just living her life day by day—taking care of her family, working at hospice, and awakening a little more each year to a deeper belief in Spirit. It took many years before she understood that her passion for hospice work was coming from her soul, and that it was a very important part of her soul journey.

The grief was always there, and working through it was a slow process. In the beginning, I didn't have any dreams about our daughter or any kind of communication from her. At that time, it would have been too scary for me. It took ten to twelve years for me to deal with my grief and begin to see that this whole experience with Melissa was the catalyst for finding my spiritual purpose.

Becoming a hospice nurse was the most important thing I did for myself. Over a period of time, I read several books by Dr. Elisabeth Kubler-Ross, the famous Chicago psychiatrist who first wrote about death and dying. I soon realized I had to start looking at my own grief issues. I even wrote my masters thesis on grief. I helped dying patients and their families deal with grief, and it became quite clear that I was helping myself, as well.

Finding a Spiritual Medium—24 Years Later

Twenty-four years after Melissa's death, Sandy was led to a spiritual medium. She did not go looking for this experience—instead, it found her. This event unfolded in such a way that it just had to be guided by Spirit.

Debbie, a co-worker at hospice, had a private session with a spiritual medium named Chrisley Witt. She came back from her appointment very excited, because Chrisley brought through believable messages from her loved ones in the spirit world. For months, Debbie kept urging Sandy to schedule a private session with Chrisley, and she finally acquiesced. Sandy spoke about her session with the medium.

> *I only went to please Debbie. It was one of the best things I ever did. I didn't tell Mike I was going because I thought he would make fun of me. He was a war planner, and he just wasn't into this kind of stuff.*

> *I walked into the room and Chrisley said, "Melissa is here." I remember reeling back like somebody had punched me. It was the first time that anyone had connected with her.*

> *By the end of the hour I was stunned because this guy knew things he had no way of knowing. I'd made a list of questions on a piece of paper before going to the session. Chrisley answered all the questions, in order, without ever seeing the paper. I purposely didn't show that list to anyone. I'm telling you, it was mind-blowing!*

Sandy had a tape of the session, so she shared it with Mike when he came home from work. Mike was shocked and amazed that their spirit daughter could send them a message. He was so intrigued with what he heard that he wanted to meet this man who knew things he had no logical way of knowing. This tape ignited a great sense of curiosity within Mike; the feeling was so strong he couldn't ignore it. He didn't know it at the time, but this intense curiosity was a call from his soul saying, "Pay attention to this. Wake up. Listen with your heart instead of your logical mind."

Kelly's Moment of Spiritual Awakening

Kelly also listened to her mother's tape and decided she wanted her own private reading with Chrisley. Kelly admits that she went into the session doubting that anyone could really deliver messages from deceased loved ones. However, she wanted to see what this was all about since her mother had such a life-changing experience with this man.

Chrisley began the session saying, "Melissa is here with us." At that very second, Kelly heard a sharp whistling sound that permeated the whole room. Chrisley continued, "That's Melissa. Your sister is a guardian angel for you. She has been around you all your life." This information confirmed what Kelly had always believed about Melissa.

Melissa and I are definitely connected even though she died two year before I was born. It's strange how I always felt like I've known her—just like I know my living sister, Maryann. As a little girl, I would tell my friends I had a sister named Melissa, and I would get very emotional. I have always felt like she is right here with me.

This hour was definitely a life-changing event for Kelly, and she came out of this session a firm believer in the possibility of spirit communication. She still sometimes listens to the tape of her first communication from Melissa, and the whistling sound can be heard very clearly. This tape serves as a reminder that the experience of connecting with Melissa's spirit was real—she didn't dream it. It's very common for people to deny their own experience when something happens that does not fit into their current definition of reality. Kelly had the wisdom to believe her experience and then to expand her definition of reality.

The Meditation Circle

After the first visit from Melissa, Mike and Sandy had an intense desire to learn about spirit communication. This desire inspired them to invite Chrisley to teach a weekly class in their home. Mike and Sandy gathered a group of twenty close friends and family members to make up the meditation circle. Their daughters Maryann, age twenty-six, and Kelly, age twenty-two, joined the group and attended these classes each week. Their thirty-year-old son, Michael, who lived in Florida, also came when he was in town. It was a real family affair!

One evening each week, Chrisley Witt led the group for three hours. He taught about life after death, spirit communication, meditation practices, angels, and life on the other side of the veil. Each week, the group members spent time developing their intuition and learning the skills to receive direct communication from Spirit. At first, progress was quite slow, and results were minimal, so they all had to have faith that they would eventually develop their psychic abilities.

Kelly was especially intrigued with all the group activities; this was not something she did to please her parents. Indeed, Kelly had a burning passion for learning about spirit communication and all of the other spiritual principles Chrisley was teaching. She grabbed the brass ring, so to speak, and took this opportunity to expand her beliefs and her abilities to tune in to the spirit world. Kelly soon discovered she had a natural talent for communicating with spirits, and indeed, found it easy, fun, and exhilarating.

Visitations From Melissa

Melissa started coming through quite often during the meditation group. Kelly had a strong connection to her sister's spirit and would usually be the first to announce, "Melissa is here! I can feel Melissa!" Sometimes Kelly and her mother would sense Melissa's presence at the same time; then they both would get very emotional.

Sandy described the circumstances that opened the door for everyone to receive communication from Melissa.

The group was so close we all felt like family. We also did exercises to increase our feeling of love as we sat in the group. We would do these visualizations to send the love energy all around the circle. We were all very connected, so this energy flowed naturally; you could just feel it. I'm sure Melissa came to this group because she could feel the love vibration pierce the veil and connect right to her heart.

Mike was in their living room meditating with the group when Melissa first came to him. It was a mystical moment he will always remember.

Melissa first showed herself to me as a young woman. She looked a lot like Kelly—red hair, very pretty, and a little taller than Kelly. I was surprised that she appeared all grown up. I kept wondering, "How could this be? She was just a baby."

When she talks to me, I hear actual words, like a regular person is talking. I use my spiritual hearing, so if you were in the room, you probably wouldn't hear anything. Her voice sounds very much like Kelly's voice.

Guidance to Open a Healing Center

About a year after starting the meditation group, Sandy woke up one morning and said to herself, "Oh, my God, we have to clear out all the antiques in the back room and create a healing center in that space." She didn't know where this idea was coming from, but she had a feeling that they had to do it.

When Sandy shared this inspiration with Mike, he responded, "Yes, you're right." Inwardly, he was wondering why he had said that.

Sandy wanted to sell the antiques to a dealer who would just take everything rather than selling their inventory off piece by piece. For three or four months, they tried to find a buyer to no avail. Finally, Sandy said a prayer, "God, if this is coming from You, You better help us."

The next day the phone rang, and a dealer called out of the blue saying he would take everything they had. And so the center was born. Mike and Sandy opened the doors without doing any advertising. Sandy explained how this unfolded.

> *We just asked God to bring us the people who needed to come. People just keep finding us. Our classes for learning meditation and spiritual healing are always full. People often come here in crisis because of a divorce, loss of job, or loss of health. All the things they've been doing in life just aren't working anymore. They're at the point of spiritual awakening and saying, "There's got to be something more to life."*

Sandy continued to work as a hospice nurse while she and Mike developed The Center of Light and Serenity. It was an easy transition to move the weekly meditation group from their living room to the new space dedicated to the healing center.

It Was All Meant to Be

In the early months of the meditation group, Sandy would get only a knowing about Melissa's presence; she could feel her love. That was all. She can still vividly recall the first time she felt more than a presence. It just happened one day after she'd been in the meditation group for about a year.

> *The first message I got from Melissa was when I was meditating alone. I didn't hear any words; it was more like feeling her presence and having clear thoughts come into my mind—thoughts that I would never think on my own. So the message came like that.*
>
> *I asked Melissa, "Why did you choose to suffer so? Why did you stay for such a short time?"*
>
> *Melissa told me very clearly that this was something that she needed to go through and that we had agreed to help her. I got the message that we had all agreed to this before we ever came here. She thanked us for allowing her to do what she needed to do. She was very grateful that we allowed her to use us so she could create the experience she needed.*

This message helped me understand that our relationship was a two-way street—she did what she needed to do, and we did what we needed to do. Once I received this message, I was able to say, "I understand and it's okay."

Since that first message, I've asked Melissa several times about the purpose of her short life here on earth. All she says to me is, "Someday you'll understand it all." So I guess it's not important for me to know at this time. I just have to trust that we all accomplished our prearranged intentions. I've come to understand the intentions for Mike and me, but I'm still curious about Melissa's intentions.

I didn't realize it at the time, but I got it later that Melissa was just passing through. I didn't understand this until I started learning about the soul journey. I feel she left us the moment she was born. She was not of this world, and I could feel she had no connection to it. My sense was that she didn't really want to stay.

Melissa wasn't bonded to me that much. I was bonded to her, but she wasn't bonded to me. I looked into her eyes and there was this distance. It was very different from our other two babies. Melissa had what I now call a "disconnect." She had it from the moment she was born.

Sandy found great comfort in the idea that Melissa's birth and death had a greater purpose. It warmed her heart and soothed her soul to know that everything unfolded according to their agreed-upon intentions because Melissa needed this experience for her own soul journey. This way of viewing their daughter's death answered the "why" questions that had plagued Sandy for twenty-five years. Viewing the situation with soul eyes, Sandy could see that it was all meant to be.

Mike also received a similar message from their spirit daughter. Mike had let go of his heart connection to Melissa when she was only three months old. As Sandy's bond grew stronger, he purposely distanced himself. Years later, he still worried he had done something wrong and carried a lot of guilt, so he asked Melissa's spirit about this.

Melissa told me that I'd done the right thing. She said it was necessary at the time for me to be that way because of what Sandy was going through. She made me understand that her birth and death were a natural thing. It was something that had to happen because she, as a soul, needed to go through this experience.

This message from Melissa's spirit helped Mike release any last bits of baggage he was carrying about this issue. It also brought him profound peace to view Melissa's birth and death with soul vision and see the bigger picture. This new perspective about Melissa's soul needs promoted Mike's spiritual growth and allowed him to find new meaning in the experience of losing their beloved baby. This spiritual answer to his "why" questions allowed Mike to release any unresolved anger at God and heal his grief at a deeper level.

Tiamo: The Master Angel of Love

One night in the meditation class, Mike saw an angel who then spoke to him. Because he was using his spiritual senses, the others in the group were unaware of the angel's presence. Mike described how this angel came to be in his life.

Chrisley, our spiritual teacher, made his transition after working with our meditation group for several years. He then came through the veil and carried on conversations with me for a year and a half. His purpose was to impart spiritual knowledge.

During his last visit, Chrisley said, "Mike, I have taught you all that I can, but now someone greater than I (in terms of knowledge) will come to you to continue with these teachings." With that, a spirit appeared to me and explained that he was the one who Chrisley had predicted would come. He also told me that he was an angel—a Master Angel of Love under the hierarchy of Michael, the Archangel.

I asked this angel for a name, and he said, "Names are not important on this side of the veil, but you can call me Tiamo, if you wish." I learned later that Tiamo means "I love you" in Italian.

Tiamo described the hierarchy of the angel kingdom and how he is known as a Master Angel of Love. He also taught us that there are angels for everything. You can have an angel for anything you want. They come and go in our lives depending on what our needs are at the time.

Angels are androgynous, but they appear to us in whatever way will be easiest for us to accept them. Tiamo comes to me as a male, probably because I was more likely to accept the idea of communicating with an angel who appeared in a masculine form. To me, he looks like Fabio, a popular male model with shoulder length blonde hair and a beautiful male physique. We've had other people at our healing center report that Tiamo comes to them, too, but for some he appears as a female.

The meditation group met for six years, and Tiamo continued to appear to Mike regularly at the meetings, as well as during his daily meditation practice. They had long conversations, and Mike began to keep a journal with all the spiritual wisdom he received from Tiamo. Eventually, Mike began sending this information out via email to a network of more than two thousand people. He considers it part of his spiritual purpose to get Tiamo's message of love out to the world. (www.SoulSoothersOnline.com)

Mike also described how Tiamo assists with spirit communication from the family relatives on the other side.

We were at my mother's wake, and I started seeing all these spirits descending from above. I first saw Tiamo come in with his hands raised to the heavens. Then my mother and a whole bunch of deceased relatives descended as if they were floating down on an invisible hand. I didn't even recognize some of these relatives. Melissa was there, as well as my dad and grandparents. It was like they were at a big party. They were all just standing around talking to each other, laughing, and using hand gestures like we do.

After a while my mother came out of the group to say goodbye. She threw kisses at everyone, and then she moved back into the group. I was watching this unfold, and then I saw Tiamo raise his arms up like an orchestra conductor. All my family members just froze, and they floated up as a group and disappeared—Melissa included.

I was so thrilled to see Melissa at the wake. Tiamo later explained to me why we often notice Melissa's presence at family times. When we gather on occasions like Christmas, weddings, and funerals, our family love raises our vibration, and it is easier for us to sense our connection with her spirit.

Tiamo Talks About Love

During our interview, Mike explained his understanding of the difference between human love and divine love.

When we are human beings in the physical world, we deal with earth-based love. We live in a family situation where our love for family members is stronger than our love for those outside the family. We feel many different love vibrations based on our different relationships with people here on earth.

Tiamo tells us that these notions about earth-based love do not exist in the spiritual world. The angels, spirit guides, and our loved ones in Spirit deal with divine love rather than earth-based love. Divine love has a much higher frequency and a different set of rules. Spirits know we are all one, and they love everyone equally. Consequently, there is no jealousy or hatred—only love.

Kelly's Relationship With Melissa

For six years, Kelly participated in the weekly meditation group, fulfilling her ongoing desire to keep improving her intuitive abilities. Over the years, she developed a very active dream life and a gift for remembering her dreams. Many of these dreams were about sharing time with Melissa in the spirit world.

I have a lot of dreams where Melissa takes me out; we go on trips through the spirit world. I remember one where we visited this beautiful garden with magnificent flowers everywhere. It was the most exquisite beauty I've ever seen! The colors were very bright and luminescent. We were moving through the garden, but we weren't worried about stepping on the flowers because we were sort of flying instead of walking.

I woke from this dream feeling very peaceful and happy. I couldn't care less if I was anywhere else. I was just so happy being with Melissa in the spirit world. I'm so thankful I have these experiences. They're very precious to me.

Over time, Kelly's ability to receive spirit communication evolved to a very high level, and she learned to have ongoing conversations with Melissa.

It's been many years since I first sensed Melissa's presence in our meditation circle. I know Melissa is always around me, and I talk to her every day. It's almost like talking to myself. I use her like a sounding board, and I ask her for guidance.

I'm getting ready to compete in a big athletic event, and I'm quite nervous about it. So as I walk on my treadmill, I say in my mind, "Melissa, you've got to be there with me." And I hear her say to me, "I'll be right there for you." I actually hear the words as if she is walking beside me, speaking. I'm absolutely sure she'll be there with me. Knowing this gives me an extra boost of confidence.

Whatever I'm doing in my life, Melissa is present, talking to me and giving me guidance. She says things like, "I'm here for you. Go for it! I'll do it with you." No matter how bad my day is, I know I'm not alone. Melissa's presence comforts me and helps me take risks in life.

I've always been a risk taker, but I don't worry because I have Melissa guiding me. I like to be a social butterfly, ride motorcycles, and compete in sporting events. I have this confident feeling that Melissa won't let anything bad happen to me. We do everything together, and we have this great psychic connection. We even look alike. Whenever I see her, she looks just like me. She even changes as I change.

Kelly and Melissa have a very twin-like relationship even though Kelly is in the physical world and Melissa is in the spirit world. Their strong heart bond has obviously pierced the veil between these two domains.

Special Guests at a Family Wedding

At age thirty, Kelly fell in love with a young man named Brandon, and they had a beautiful wedding in the Bahamas. The whole family gathered on the beach watching their romantic ceremony. The wedding party was inside a gazebo near the edge of the water, and all the family members were seated just outside. Mike described the mystical moment when his spiritual vision opened to the higher vibrations of the spirit world.

I was sitting there watching my daughter Kelly and Brandon standing in the gazebo with the minister. Suddenly, I began to see our family members in Spirit standing in the midst of the wedding attendants. I could see them just like I see you today.

Kelly's deceased grandparents stood behind her, and Brandon's deceased sister Lisa stood next to him. Then Melissa came and took her place right beside Kelly. Tiamo was standing directly behind Kelly and Brandon with his arms outstretched, as if he were embracing them from behind.

It was so beautiful to see! Melissa looked at Kelly so lovingly—as if she had known Kelly and been around her all her life. It was just so awesome that tears just started coming to my eyes.

Then I had to tell Sandy and the groom's mother what I was crying about. So pretty soon everyone knew that Melissa, Brandon's sister

Lisa, Kelly's grandparents, and Tiamo were present for this very special occasion. It was such a joyful wedding, and here we were all crying!

Kelly's Spiritual Purpose

Now at age thirty-two, Kelly has a clear vision of merging her career with her spiritual purpose.

My heart's desire is to do something that makes a difference—like grief counseling and helping people connect with the spirits of their loved ones. I want to make spirit communication my life's work. I feel passionate about doing it, even though I don't know exactly how it will unfold. Right now, I just know where I want to end up.

A lot of my friends ask my advice when they feel stuck in life. I just give them what comes to me from Spirit. Even in high school, my friends would ask me to help them write a letter to smooth out a relationship. They would say, "You always know the right words." I just tell them what Spirit tells me.

I guess you could say I've had this psychic gift my whole life. I never used to trust my instincts. Chrisley had a big effect on me because he taught me to have confidence in my spiritual senses. Now, I know that I can rely on what I see and hear from the spirit beings. I have always received information from Spirit; I just didn't know that was the source.

There's a young girl at my workplace whose fiancé committed suicide. I didn't know her very well, but I attended the funeral. As I was sitting there quietly listening to the church music, I began to get messages from her fiancé. There were no words—it was more like thoughts imprinted on my mind.

So after the service, I told her what I'd heard her fiancé say, only I didn't have the courage to tell her that I was receiving messages from his spirit; I didn't want to scare her. So I just said, "You know he loves you. If he could take this back, he would because he wants to be with you and your children. You just need to remember how much he loved you and your children. His love will always be with you."

When I get these kinds of messages, I know it's not me. I can feel the energy of the spirit communicating with me; I can even feel if the vibration is male or female. Somehow, I just know the difference.

Since her first encounter with Melissa over eleven years ago, Kelly has followed her passion to learn more and more about spirit communication. She practices daily to fine tune her skills and enhance her natural gift of receiving messages from Melissa and other spirits. Kelly has raised her consciousness so that she is now a very skilled spiritual medium who can deliver inspiring messages from the spirit world to family and friends; she just doesn't do it professionally—yet.

Prearranged Intentions

The interviews for this story took place forty years after Melissa's birth and death. Sandy has an enlightened view of her spiritual journey that unfolded during this time.

In retrospect, working at hospice prepared me for believing in life after death, communicating with Melissa, and finding my spiritual purpose to become a healer and create the center with Mike.

This grieving mother found her way on her spiritual journey by following an inner urge to become a hospice nurse. Remember that she stated, "It was a passion I couldn't deny." As she listened to her heart, Sandy's spiritual evolution led her from her roles as wife, mother, and homemaker to hospice nurse and then spiritual healer.

Likewise, Mike took his first steps on his spiritual path by following his passion to learn to communicate with their spirit baby after Melissa delivered her first message through Chrisley Witt. This passion was the catalyst for Mike to evolve from a war logistics planner to a spiritual medium who could easily communicate with not only his daughter, but also other powerful spirits like Tiamo. He continued on his journey by becoming a healer and opening the center.

As this book goes to press, Mike and Sandy spend their time working together in The Center of Light and Serenity. As they evolve, so does the center. Sandy became certified in reflexology, hypnotherapy, and aromatherapy. She eventually let go of her position at hospice to work full time as a healer in the center. Mike and Sandy, both Reiki Masters, jointly lead classes in this ancient method of spiritual healing. They originally thought their work would be to bring about physical healings, but they soon found their main focus was healing the spirit. Sandy explained:

Unless the spirit is healed, nothing else can be healed. You have to get to the underlying cause of a physical illness. Our work is much more than having people receive psychic readings. We teach our clients to use their own intuitive abilities to get their own answers from within.

The Center of Light and Serenity is definitely guided by unseen forces. Mike and Sandy have never advertised, yet people from all walks of life find their way to the center. Many medical professionals come wanting to learn about spiritual healing and holistic medicine. The Reiki classes are filled with nurses who want to learn how the human energy field influences the physical body. Doctors, chiropractors, and nutritionists also attend classes and do their own work for personal growth and spiritual development.

Points to Ponder

This story bears witness to the soul growth of three family members as each continues on his or her individual, yet connected, sacred path of spiritual evolution after the death of Melissa, their beloved baby. Mike and Sandy are ordinary people who, for the first twenty-four years after their infant's death, have no conscious connection to their spirit daughter. During this time, Sandy finds her soul work of becoming a hospice nurse, even though she is unaware of the guidance and inspiration she is receiving from Melissa. This grieving mother is eventually led to sit with a spiritual medium, and Melissa uses this opportunity to send a dramatic wake-up call to her parents and her younger sister.

After this defining moment, Mike, Sandy, and Kelly discover they each have a passion for learning to communicate with their beloved spirit baby; this becomes the driving force for them to organize a meditation group that meets weekly for six years. After months of instruction and dedicated practice, these three committed spiritual seekers learn the skills of spirit communication and open their minds and hearts to Melissa, who becomes a very wise teacher and guide. *So we see that Melissa, a baby who lived only seven months, becomes the catalyst for the spiritual awakening of her parents and her sister Kelly. And we also see that Melissa, like the Inca spirit babies, brings profound healing to her family.*

Mike, Sandy, and Kelly have an unshakable belief that their lives have unfolded according to the soul agreements they made with Melissa before any of them came to earth. To put it simply, they believe it was all meant to be. Both Mike and Sandy receive messages from their spirit daughter indicating that her death was not an accident—rather, as Mike says in the story, *"It was something that had to happen because, as a soul, Melissa needed to go through this experience."* These evolved parents do not yet know exactly why Melissa planned to come to their family and stay in the physical for such a short time, but they understand it was for her soul growth.

I invite you to stretch your beliefs about the spiritual purpose of your beloved baby's death. *Can you trust that, like Melissa and her family, you had a soul agreement with your baby before you all came to earth? Can you believe your journey through grief is meant to be? Can you embrace the idea that you agreed to this difficult journey for your own spiritual evolution? And finally, can you trust that your spirit baby also agreed to join your family for a very short time for the purpose of his or her own soul growth?*

Once you are able to shift to a spiritual perspective and answer yes to all of these questions, your quest to heal your grief will expand into a sacred journey of spiritual evolution.

CHAPTER SEVEN

The Gift of Spiritual Awakening

*You all agreed to come to earth together
to learn certain spiritual lessons.
Dylan loved you so much that he called on
all this protection and support
so you could learn the lessons and not be devastated.*
—*Debbie, Messenger for Dylan*

Mark and Beth were so thrilled to hear the news, "You're pregnant!" They'd been dealing with the ongoing frustrations of infertility issues for six years of their twelve-year marriage. Finally, with this announcement, their struggle was behind them, and their hearts were bursting with exquisite joy, love, and excitement for the new baby who was coming to join their family. In a word, they were euphoric!

Then at sixteen weeks, during a routine ultrasound, the technician got very quiet and said, "I have to go get the doctor." For Mark and Beth these words marked the beginning of a very long journey into the unknown—a journey filled with great fear, dread, and grief, as well as tremendous hope, faith, and love.

Below, Beth tells the story of her spiritual awakening as she went through the rest of the pregnancy and the devastating loss of their infant son.

A Devastating Diagnosis

At our sixteen-week ultrasound, the doctors could tell our baby's heart was pushed over to the side, but they didn't know why. After further testing, they diagnosed our infant as having a congenital diaphragmatic hernia. We learned that our baby's diaphragm had a hole in it while all the organs were forming. This hole allowed the organs to move up into the chest area, thus pushing the heart out of place. The doctors explained, "The worst problem is that the lungs now don't have space to develop normally. We won't know the extent of the problems until your baby is born because his lungs won't show up on an ultrasound taken while he's still in the womb. Your baby has a fifty-fifty chance of surviving."

Our twenty-four-week wait was very challenging, to say the least. I couldn't go around thinking this baby was going to die. Dylan was connected to me physically, so I felt I needed to stay positive and do everything I could to help him be healthy. I also wanted to enjoy this time of being pregnant. It was very, very hard. The hardest thing I've ever done!

Talking to Dylan in the Womb

Originally, we didn't want to know the sex of the baby. However, once we knew there was a problem, not knowing was just one more thing that was out of our control. So we found out our little one was a boy and named him Dylan. Knowing he was a boy and calling him by his name in the womb helped us connect more deeply with him.

Early in the pregnancy, somebody told me it was important to talk to your baby in the womb, so that's what we did. The whole time I was pregnant I had this ongoing conversation with Dylan about whatever I was doing. It always felt very natural. Sometimes I spoke out loud, and other times I talked to him in my mind. For example, I would laugh and say to him, "Mommy is making an omelet for breakfast, and then you are going to get some of it when I eat it."

We talked to Dylan even more after we found he had a problem. We just talked to him all the time! Before a trip to the doctor's office I'd tell our son, "Okay, Dylan, we're going to the doctor's office. We're going to have another ultrasound, so we can see what you look like." In addition, we kept telling our son how much we loved him. We couldn't say it often enough.

Dylan the Teacher

My sister Barbara is a very spiritual woman. She called one day when I was about six months pregnant to just check in and see how things were going. I told her some of the lessons I was learning through the experience of carrying a baby who had only a fifty-fifty chance of living: "I'm learning all this anatomy and medicine. I'm learning to be patient. I'm learning I have no control."

Then Barbara announced so matter-of-factly, "Oh, Dylan is a wise old soul. He's here to be a teacher." I wasn't thinking on that level at all yet, so I responded, "Why do you say that?" She replied, "Are you listening to yourself? Would you be learning any of these things if it weren't for Dylan?" I said quietly, "No. I guess not." I didn't think about that conversation until after Dylan died. Then I realized she was right—Dylan was here to be a teacher.

Dylan's Transition: A Time of Love

Dylan lived exactly two weeks before making his transition. He spent the entire time in the NICU hooked up to life support to keep his little body alive. Mark and I continued our usual routine of talking to our son constantly. The nurses told us, "He's able to recognize your voices because he's heard you talking to him all these months. All of his vital signs stabilize when he hears you. It's very calming for him." That was wonderful for us to know! Even though we didn't do much of the actual care in the hospital, we were able to calm and soothe our son because he recognized our voices. It brought a bit of joy to our grieving hearts that he knew we were there.

The entire two weeks we stayed by his bedside talking to him, reading him stories, and reassuring him of our love. We were totally focused on our infant son—every thought, every feeling was about him. We essentially put our lives on hold because nothing else mattered in the moment. Reflecting back, I now understand we were learning to "be present." Those weeks with Dylan are still the most precious time for us as a family.

We knew we were going to take Dylan off life support on the fourteenth day. We spent the previous night with our son and talked to him continually, just like we had since he came into my womb. Our tears fell silently as we told our son: "You're going to heaven. You won't be alone there because you will be with Grandpa and Grandma Seyda, and Grandma Frida. Our friends Phil and Rob will be with you, too. They all love you and will be watching over you. And it would be really great if you could send us some kind of sign to let us know that you're okay."

The next morning, Mark and I held our precious baby as they disconnected the machines. It was so incredibly wonderful to hold him! *Pachelbel's Canon in D*, which was always soothing to him, was playing in the background as we held him close. Dylan died in our arms, and we actually heard the last breath that he took. It was so very peaceful and beautiful. It really made me think about my death and how, at that sacred time, I want to be in the arms of someone who loves me.

First Signs From Dylan

The day after Dylan's death, Mark and I both felt the need to do something to de-stress and rejuvenate. We'd been living in the NICU for two weeks, so the idea of walking outside amidst the trees felt really great. We drove twenty minutes to get to our favorite forest preserve and began walking.

Immediately we felt quite uncomfortable. There was an energy around us that made us feel we were in the wrong place—like we were supposed to go somewhere else. It was a very intuitive thing. Strangely, Mark and I both felt it. Rather quickly, we started sharing this feeling and decided to leave.

Driving towards home, we simultaneously noticed another park that was new to both of us. We pulled in and parked the car. As we looked around, we were drawn to a particular walking path. It led us to a river where some big, flat boulders made a platform out into the moving water. We walked out on the boulders and sat watching the flow of the river for quite a while. This time the place felt right. The combination of the boulders, the rushing water, and the fall sun coming through the trees was very healing.

Finally, we stood up to leave with the intention of continuing along the walking path. Then the strangest thing happened. I was about to take a step towards the path, and while my leg was in midair, an unknown force turned my body ninety degrees. It felt like "someone" physically nudged me to take a different direction; although this force was actually pretty strong, it was also very gentle.

I suddenly found myself walking further out on the boulders towards the river. After taking only a few steps, I looked down, and there was a penny lying in plain sight. Right there in the middle of the wilderness, we found a bright, shiny, new penny! We both went, "Hmmm. This is interesting."

We picked up the penny in a bit of a daze and walked back to the car. Mark turned on the ignition, and the radio started playing *Pachelbel's Canon in D*, the last song we played for Dylan. We both burst out crying! We cried out joyously to our son, "Thank you, Dylan. We got the penny and we got the music. Thank you for letting us know you are okay."

I know why Dylan used a penny to send us a sign. My husband is a runner and during my pregnancy, he started picking up change he found while running on the road. Usually it was pennies. Each time I told Dylan, "Daddy found another penny, and we're putting it in the bank for you." So of course, our spirit son knew this penny would touch our hearts and remind us of all those previous times we told him about finding a penny.

Looking back, I realize we would have missed Dylan's penny completely had we continued the journey Mark and I planned that day. Spirit actually intervened so we could find this special sign from our spirit son. I feel so blessed to have such strong guidance. Ten years later, pennies from Dylan still keep showing up. Each one ignites a poof of love energy in my heart and reminds me of our eternal connection.

Devastating Grief

The first days, weeks, and months after Dylan's death our grief was excruciating; it literally permeated our thoughts, our feelings—our whole existence. Mark and I were both physically and emotionally exhausted from those two weeks in the NICU, but we couldn't sleep. We couldn't focus on anything, but we didn't care either. Our ways of dealing with our grief were similar, which was a blessing. While I was able to take off six weeks from work, Mark went back to his job in just two weeks. It was a very hard time for us.

We were really good to each other during those dark, initial days of grief. If we were both having a bad day, we just held each other and cried. If I had a slightly better day than Mark, I would hold him. On another day, if he was the stronger one, he would hold me. We really supported each other through those first months.

My body was literally filled with pain during my early grief experience, especially my chest area. It truly felt like my heart was physically broken. I knew it was going to be awful, and I knew I would be crying, but these physical symptoms were quite a surprise. I had had other losses and gone through grief, but it was nothing like this. This was truly the first loss that affected me so deeply.

People really wanted to help, and so many did reach out to us. I liked it best when people just did things for us without our asking—like run errands or bring food. Everybody was offering to do things for us but it was hard to go back and ask for their help. I kept thinking that I should be able to go to the grocery store and cook simple meals. It wasn't like I had some physical injury or a sickness that prevented me from doing these household chores. But all of the everyday chores took so much energy, and I didn't have any—not even an ounce.

A friend told me that grief was far more crippling than any physical injury even though nobody could see the damage from Dylan's death. This made me think, "What does this grief feel like to me? If I had to describe it in physical terms, what would I say?" Finally, the perfect image came to me. It felt like a hundred six-foot sabers were stabbed into my heart when Dylan died—half of each sword in front of me, the other half sticking out my back. Three months after his death, they were still there, with blood continuing to gush from each of my wounds.

Once I had that horrific image of myself, it became clear why I was having such a difficult time trying to do everyday things. I finally understood it was insane that I expected myself to function normally. After this awareness, I became better at accepting help when people offered it.

I have often wished that others could feel my pain and see all the swords through my heart. I believe that if they could, they wouldn't say or do such insensitive things like suggesting another baby would help my grief, or saying nothing and acting like Dylan was never here. Even a year after Dylan's death, I found myself thinking, "If people could see the swords, they would also see that some of them are still piercing my heart. And whenever the swords are finally gone, they will see the massive scar that remains on my chest, right over my heart."

I've come to the conclusion that only those who have eyes to see the swords will be able to truly understand the impact Dylan's life and death has had on me—I will never be the same. I am forever changed.

Talking to Dylan in Spirit

After Dylan died, I was making an omelet one morning, and I found myself talking to him as I had when he was in my womb. Of course, I just started bawling when I realized that he wasn't alive anymore. But then I thought, "You know what? I'm just going to keep talking to him."

It was very healing for me to talk to Dylan and believe that he was present. I didn't feel like I was getting any kind of message from him, but it just felt good to keep chatting away. It's been ten years since Dylan died, and I still talk to him every day; I've just never stopped. I will probably always talk to him. I don't feel his presence all the time, but I know he is around when I need him.

Looking back, I'm so grateful people told me about communicating with our baby in the womb. After Dylan's transition, talking to our spirit baby and believing he could hear me was the beginning of my spiritual transformation.

A Little Tug

Mark had another brief moment of spiritual connection with Dylan about a month after our son's transition. Here are his words about that event.

I was lying in bed one night and was awakened when "somebody" gave me a little tug on my heel. At the same time, I heard a whispered, "I love you." It all happened so quickly! Of course I thought of Dylan immediately. I'd like to think it was a sign from our son, and yet sometimes I doubt. For a long time I kept hoping it would happen again, but it hasn't. It was certainly very comforting in the moment.

In the beginning, Mark and I were completely focused on feeling the connection to Dylan. Events like finding the penny, hearing *Pachelbel's Canon in D* on the car radio, and Mark's dream were kind of an introduction for us—a little nudge to begin exploring further into spiritual matters. At this time, we were oblivious to the bigger spiritual picture. You might say we had no clue!

Feeling a Presence

In spite of the dire predictions about our baby, I had to believe Dylan was going to come home with us. I couldn't bear the thought of not preparing his room or not being ready for him. So we had Dylan's room decorated and set up as a nursery just as if everything was okay. After Dylan died, we kept his room as it was—we had just completed everything the week before he arrived. We had Dylan cremated and kept his ashes in a little wooden box that we put in his crib. I often found moments of serenity "just being" in his beautiful room.

In the first months after Dylan's death, once or twice a week, I would often wake up in the middle of the night and be unable to get back to sleep. It was my first experience with insomnia. After many nights of tossing and turning, I discovered that going to my son's room would soothe my aching heart. I found it comforting to take his ashes and rock them and talk to him. I said these simple messages again and again: "Mommy and Daddy love you, Dylan. We really miss you. We just love you so much." Of course, I was sobbing profusely as I poured out my heart in the night. Then, after a huge release, I'd become peaceful and feel calm enough to resume sleeping in my own bed for the rest of the night.

At some point, I started noticing something around me when I was rocking—it seemed like a presence, but I didn't really know what to make of it. Often, I also felt a definite pressure on my shoulders—like someone was standing behind me and putting their hands there. It wasn't scary or anything. I was aware that it happened every time I rocked in Dylan's room with his ashes in my lap. At the time, I didn't necessarily connect it with Dylan. I just felt it and noticed it; that was all.

A Comforting Dream

We requested an autopsy so we could further understand what had happened to Dylan. The report was ready the week before Christmas, but we decided to wait until after the holidays to meet with the doctor. We knew sitting through the autopsy report was going to be tough—a friend who is a nurse prepared us for it being cold and clinical. Naturally, we were quite anxious about the whole thing. The morning we were scheduled for this very difficult meeting, I had a Dylan dream. It was short and vivid—a dream from Spirit.

> *Mark and I entered an examining room in a doctor's office, and there was our Dylan on the table. His eyes were closed, and he was perfectly still. The doctor took out a scalpel and was going to start cutting our son open, doing the autopsy right there in front of us. I stopped him, saying, "Dylan is not dead. You cannot do this autopsy."*
>
> *A lively discussion ensued about whether Dylan was dead or not. Finally, we all agreed that he had died. Our son was lying on his stomach facing me. Just as the doctor was about to make an incision, Dylan opened one eye, winked at me, smiled, closed his eye, and went back to appearing lifeless. It happened as quickly as a flash! No one else saw it. I calmly and quietly said to myself, "Oh, Dylan's not dead." And then the dream ended!*

I woke up feeling a little shaken that, in the dream, I was just about to see an autopsy performed on our baby. This message from Spirit reminded me that what we were going to do later that day was only about Dylan's physical body, that indeed, a part of Dylan, his spirit, was still alive. It's no surprise that this dream picked up on some of my struggles with the physical and spiritual aspects of death. To this day, I'm so grateful to Dylan for sending this reminder. Now I keep telling myself, "Our baby is not dead."

Another Teacher Appears

There's an old saying, "When the student is ready the teacher appears." Indeed, this was true for me—the perfect spiritual teacher appeared even though I was not consciously looking for one. It happened in a very synchronistic way.

My sister Mary Jean lives close by and was an incredible support for us while Dylan was in the NICU. A month after our son's death, she attended a small house party where she met Debbie, a little-known spiritual medium. Debbie first spoke to the whole group and then did little fifteen-minute private readings. Feeling both excitement and trepidation, Mary Jean grabbed a private session. Thankfully, she taped this session so I could hear the message delivered that night by this gifted medium.

This wonderful being came to this planet for such a short time to complete one last earth lesson for himself. He also came to bring the opportunity for many lessons to his parents, and to you, and to other souls who have been touched by him and who have loved him deeply.

One of the important memories or awarenesses that this soul offers is love in the present moment. He sends this message: "Let the present moment be the fullness that it can be."

Another lesson is the absolute truth in Spirit that love never goes away, it never dies. This child is really a very large and wise spirit. This being is no more dead than you or I. The consciousness lives! This unique presence is still alive and is still able to communicate.

Please tell his mother and father that he hears what they say to him. When the tears are less for them, they will be able to hear what he says to them.

I must say that listening to my sister's tape was a moment of awakening for me. I already knew about psychics and mediums, but I was never interested. It was just not on my radar screen. However, after hearing Dylan's message, I felt compelled to call Debbie; my goal was to contact my spirit son and get my own message.

A Huge Awakening

A month later, with great anticipation, I sat with Debbie for a private session. My heart pounded with excitement, not fear. This was a huge step for me since I'd never done anything like this before. Perhaps it was easier for me to take this step because Dylan's death just cracked me wide open. I felt like my heart broke, but the good thing was that it was now unlocked. This way of opening was incredibly painful, yet it also allowed good things to flow in—like Debbie.

Debbie began our session by saying some beautiful prayers and calling all the spirits beings to gather. She called in my guides and angels, her guides and angels, and Dylan's spirit, as well as his guides and angels. I immediately felt the same presence and the exact pressure on my shoulders that I always felt while rocking my son's ashes in the night.

When I described this sensation to Debbie, she announced, "That's Dylan's presence. He's touching your shoulders right now. And that is also him touching your shoulders when you rock in his room." I was absolutely thrilled to hear it! I believed her even though it had never occurred to me that Dylan's spirit could cause any kind of physical sensation. Here are the important highlights of my first session with this gifted spiritual medium:

> *Dylan's soul is being well cared for. This sweet soul spends a lot of time with the angels. He is in heavenly classes to learn the responsibilities, the commitments, and the traits of angels so that he may become one of them and bring angelic love back to this planet and other souls.*

> *Dylan says to tell you, "A soul could not have asked for a finer being than you to be my mother. I was so honored to be with you—with both of you. I felt this connection to you as a pure rush of love."*

> *Your spirit son also says to tell you, "I really admire and deeply love you for the courage that you had to let me go back to Spirit. You have done a fine job of knowing that I am back in the hands of the Creator—back where I truly belong. I am so grateful to have had this opportunity to come and be with you, even for a short amount of time. It was important—and such a gift to me—that you allowed this to happen. You allowed our souls to dance together in this time."*

> *This is a test of faith for you and Mark. When we have given the finest of ourselves and things don't turn out like we expected (or, like we had faith it would), we are so hurt and so devastated. The natural tendency is to believe that something has gone terribly wrong. We often believe there is something wrong with us or there is something wrong with God. You are doing a fine job of moving through that pain and keeping your faith.*

> *There is no punishment in this situation. This is truly a blessing of Spirit for all of you; there is no punishment or stigma attached to what's happened. It is just an opportunity for three precious and beautiful souls to grow.*

This spiritual wisdom coming from my son was an amazing, soothing balm to my terrible heartache; it was also a tremendous catalyst to begin healing my grief. In this first session, Debbie helped me make a deeper connection with Dylan's spirit. I was already getting signs, like having dreams, and feeling my spirit son's presence and his touch on my shoulders. However, it was very hard for me to trust these subtle forms of communication that were always so nebulous. This session confirmed that I was truly getting communication from our spirit son. Knowing this made my heart feel lighter.

Debbie became my spiritual counselor; I saw her every two months or so for a couple of years. Not surprisingly, she was the perfect person to guide my healing journey. Debbie was always very sweet, kind, and gentle with me—she was a huge part of my healing.

From the beginning, Debbie described Dylan as a wise old soul who was very powerful and had a purpose for his short life here on earth. She explained that my son was now a spiritual being composed of energy—she even described the many colors that make up his spirit.

This was all news to me, and, at first, it was rather shocking—it certainly didn't match my beliefs at the time. I was still thinking of Dylan as a baby in physical form. I would talk about his soul being in heaven, but I still thought about him as a little, helpless being who didn't know much and didn't have the ability to think. Debbie kept telling me, "You need to think about your son's soul and his spirit—he just came to you in the form of a baby."

It took me at least a year or more to let go of thinking of my son as a baby. After numerous sessions with Debbie, I was able to change my perception, see Dylan as a wise old soul, and forget about the physical part. This was a huge shift for me!

Protection and Support for the Journey

I scheduled a second session with Debbie about four months after Dylan's transition. Again, she brought through a key message from Spirit. In fact, this message lifted me to a whole new level—it was the catalyst for achieving a major shift in consciousness about my grief journey.

Dylan is a soul that has been your friend forever. There is such love in this dear, dear connection that has existed forever and ever. People on earth sometimes make the mistake of thinking that babies don't know anything. This soul called Dylan is so wise.

Together, you all agreed to come to earth and learn certain spiritual lessons. He loved you so much that he called on all this protection and support so you could learn the lessons and not be devastated.

He asked that you always have spiritual nourishment to help you complete the journey.

Your guides and angels are showing me "hands of light" giving you a massage all over your body while you were carrying Dylan in your womb. This was done routinely in the night, so you would have very few physical challenges with this pregnancy. The plan was for your total focus to be on connecting spiritually with Dylan, and loving and caring for him.

Of course, I was absolutely mesmerized as Debbie delivered this message from my spirit son and the angels. During the session, the vibrational level was so high that she was actually communicating directly with my soul; indeed, there was a transmission of energy that took place beyond the level of mind and human thought. I felt the truth of those words in my very heart and soul. I believe the message felt true to me because my soul remembers those ancient promises.

After this reading, I started thinking about all the ways I had been supported and protected after hearing the news that our baby might not live. Early in the process, I often seemed to be in the right place at the right time to make some very meaningful connections. For instance, I ran into a former boss, and he introduced me to his wife Sharon, who is a pediatrician. I just happened to call Sharon one day and she said, "Let me connect you with my best friend, who is a neonatal intensive care doctor here in town." Then weeks later, I "accidentally" reconnected with Helen, a friend I had known for years. Unbeknownst to me, she had previously been a NICU nurse. After hearing about Dylan, she was quite eager to join my unofficial support team.

In retrospect, it is very clear that people with medical expertise were put in my path to help me understand the medical aspects of our journey with Dylan. Looking back, I can see that it was all rather magical!

Late in the pregnancy, I was terribly nervous. After Dylan's birth, it was imperative for him to go immediately to the NICU because the doctors couldn't be sure if his lungs were developed enough for him to breathe on his own. I knew I had to be at the hospital for his delivery—I couldn't be on my way to the hospital. I kept wondering, "How will I know for sure I'm in labor? How will I know when to go to the hospital?"

About a week before Dylan's birth, I dreamed I was eight months pregnant and my water broke in the middle of the night. The dream was very brief, but it was so real that I sat up in bed and thought it really happened. Even after the dream, I still worried. A week later my water broke in the middle of the night, so I knew to go to the hospital. Amazingly, everything unfolded exactly like the dream!

I didn't quite get it at the time. After Dylan's message I understood the dream came directly from Spirit; it was sent to provide me with more support and protection. It's such a blessing that my spiritual eyes are now wide open so I can see all the miracles that took place along my healing journey. Now I know for certain I'm never alone! I feel so blessed to be aware of all these meant-to-be connections.

Looking back, I can see that spiritual nourishment seemed to appear throughout my grief journey without any effort on my part. Friends and acquaintances suggested spiritual books that brought so much guidance and understanding, as well as many "Aha!" experiences. The books just kept appearing though I didn't go to the library or the Internet to do any research.

Another meant-to-be support person was a friend named Gary; he and his wife had a baby girl who died about seven years before Dylan. I talked to him a lot because I didn't know anybody else who had gone through the experience of having a full-term baby die. His experience with his daughter was also a spiritual awakening for him, so he was able to guide me through my spiritual transformation. How wonderful to have my own personal guide for the grief journey!

At some point, Gary said to me, "Dylan has given you many wonderful gifts." Nobody had used those terms with me before. Yes, we had this incredible pain about Dylan's death, but we also had these incredible blessings. I made a pact with myself to be open to those gifts. This was a very important shift for me on the journey.

Strangely, years earlier Gary and I dated for a while, but it just didn't seem right, so we broke up and remained friends. I told Gary: "The plan was for us to connect and remain friends because you were meant to be my spiritual support after Dylan's death. We were never supposed to be together in a romantic way. You have been a huge catalyst for my spiritual awakening and seeing all of this as a sacred journey. You are such a gift to me. I am so grateful!"

Of course, it was no accident that I was also led to Debbie, the spiritual medium who could pierce the veil and bring all the awe-inspiring messages from Dylan. Sitting with this gifted woman changed my whole grief journey. After receiving these messages from my spirit son, I understood Debbie was also part of the plan for me to heal.

Raising a Spiritual Child

Our son Tyler was born four years after Dylan. This six-year-old kid has such amazing, powerful energy! He's very personable, talks to anybody, and makes everybody smile. We told Tyler about Dylan from the start, so our living son has a great connection with his spirit brother.

Mark and I both think we would have been great parents to Dylan if he had lived. And we also agreed we are even better parents to Tyler because of our spiritual awakening after Dylan went to heaven.

We are using everything we learned on our spiritual journey to raise Tyler. One of my greatest lessons is that I learned to be present and enjoy the moment. This lesson has served me well in my life—particularly with Tyler. I am really present with him, and it's been that way from the start.

After our experience with Dylan, I began reading a lot of spiritual books. Through my reading, I learned that the soul of the baby is not in the womb for some time after conception. One day, while still pregnant with Tyler, I said to Dylan and my other spirit guides, "I would really love to know when Tyler's spirit joins his little body in my womb. I want to be able to feel it."

And then it happened! I felt it! The pregnancy was about two months along when I felt this energy come in. I felt it in my heart. I just knew what it was. We were going on a trip to be with my extended family to celebrate my dad's birthday. I remember thinking, "Oh, this baby wants to make sure he is part of our big family. He doesn't want to miss connecting with everyone."

Young children are naturally very connected to the spirits and the energies of the other world. Tyler is our only living child, but he does not consider himself an only child. He often talks about his brother in heaven and even announces how old Dylan is.

I'm raising Tyler to be very spiritually aware and very connected. It's so different from the way I was raised, and it's so much fun for me as a parent. Since I've taught my son to be open, he talks easily about his brother who died. I overheard this conversation with another mother at our local pool:

> **Mother**: *Do you have any brothers or sisters?*
>
> **Tyler**: *Yes, I have a brother.*
>
> **Mother**: *Then why isn't he here at the pool?*
>
> **Tyler**: *Well, because he's dead.*

This mother was a bit shocked by Tyler, but I'm not concerned about that.

We still celebrate Dylan's birthday every year with a little ceremony at home. When Tyler was only three years old, I talked to him about his brother in heaven. For him, it was like Dylan was in Chicago. He asked: "Can we go visit him? Can we take a plane to see him? Can I walk there? Can we take a car?" Tyler was so frustrated because he really wanted the whole family to be together to celebrate Dylan's birthday.

I was trying my best to explain the concept of heaven to this three-year-old child. At some point he said, "Can I talk to him on the phone?" I answered, "No, but you can talk to him any time. He will hear you. He might come to you in your dreams. You can even ask him to come in your dreams."

Tyler has a peanut allergy, so he can't eat peanut butter. Sometimes he gets really frustrated about this restriction. When he was four years old he announced, "I can't wait until I die. I'm going to go to heaven and have a peanut butter sandwich with my brother." We've talked about it enough that he knows when you go to heaven, all your physical problems are healed. He really gets it! I find this so amazing!

Nine months after Dylan died, we had a miscarriage. It was very early in the pregnancy—like five weeks maybe, so we didn't give the baby a name, and we never really talked about this event. It was such a bittersweet thing—sad to lose another baby, but happy to know we could get pregnant again. One day I happened to mention this baby to Tyler and we had the most amazing conversation:

Tyler: *Could I name the baby?*

Mom: *Sure.*

Tyler: *I want to name the baby "Happy."*

Mom: *That's beautiful. Why do you want to name the baby Happy?*

Tyler: *Because I'm so happy I have another brother or sister in heaven.*

So he gets it! I'm so glad I'm supporting him being spiritually open and helping him understand life on a metaphysical level. Even though I know his spirit or his soul understands much more than his mind, I thought that conversation was so amazing. Tyler tells people about his brother Dylan who died and the baby named Happy. Tyler actually thinks of us as a family of five. And I'm so pleased!

When Tyler was four years old, we discovered he has some psychic abilities. College sports are really big in our town, and usually we take Tyler with us to the local college baseball games. One spring we were attending a series of games for a tournament. Before the games, Tyler began drawing pictures showing the players on different bases and the score on the scoreboard; his pictures were very detailed—even depicting the players' numbers on their shirts. The coach thought it was cute to post these pictures in the dugout at the games. After a few games, everyone started noticing that Tyler's drawings usually came true. It was astonishing! One of the players announced to us, "That's a really smart kid."

I don't know for sure how Tyler does it—he gets in a zone where he's connected to Spirit. He must be getting guidance from his angels and spirit guides about what's going to happen in the future. Maybe Dylan is also giving him some tips. Whenever Tyler starts to draw, I just leave him alone and stay out of the way. It's always fascinating to see what comes through from Spirit.

Tyler is a part of this whole spiritual deal. I believe he signed up to be part of this family knowing his older brother would die. I'm very interested to see how Tyler's going to develop. I can't wait to discover his soul purpose and understand why he is here on earth. I'm always talking to Dylan, saying, "Make sure I'm supporting Tyler with his soul purpose in the way I'm supposed to." I just know Tyler is going to have his own amazing purpose!

My Spiritual Purpose

I have this incredible passion for sharing my story with people. I've discovered that talking about Dylan is very healing for me, and it's also incredibly educating for everybody else. Once I found my story could help other grieving families I said, "This is what I will do!" And it's totally right! I know this is my purpose—it's what I'm supposed to be doing.

About six months after Dylan's death, I sent a letter about our hospital stay to his medical team. My intention was to give them feedback about our experience—both the positives and the negatives. I commented on some of the physical aspects of the hospital that were a problem for us. I didn't know it at the time, but they were in the process of planning a new facility, and they worked my suggestions into the design. Now when I go to the hospital and see all my recommendations in operation—it's mind blowing. They actually listened to me!

Ann, a colleague, and I formed an organization we named Compassionate Passages (www.compassionatepassages.org). One of our purposes is to tell people about our experiences with dying babies in the NICU. Ann is passionate about this cause because her beloved niece died in the NICU a few years after Dylan. We both realized early on that people don't talk about this topic; it's too painful, so they shove it under the rug.

Both Ann and I dedicate a lot of time to educating families and healthcare professionals about the needs of a family with a dying baby. I often go to hospitals and speak to doctors on grand rounds about this topic. Somebody always comes up to me and says, "Thank you. No one talks about these issues. We need to hear about this stuff. We don't know what to say. We don't know what to do. We don't know how to help these families." I've always gotten positive feedback for this new work. More opportunities keep showing up for Ann and me to do this work through Compassionate Passages. Of course, this is confirmation that we're on the right path.

It's no accident that I discovered a national organization called PLIDA— the Pregnancy Loss and Infant Death Alliance. This association fills a great need because there are so many people who are struggling with grief issues after infant death. During my research, I've learned that one in four pregnancies ends in a miscarriage, stillbirth, or infant death. The numbers are huge! I'm now board president of PLIDA, and this feels very "meant-to-be." I'm enjoying my new role because it fits with my purpose of helping others heal after the death of an infant.

It's been ten years since Dylan's transition, and I've just now started speaking at conferences and other meetings about my spiritual journey with my spirit son. This means going public with my "Dylan stories" of spirit communication and the deeper spiritual lessons I've learned on my healing journey. Debbie, my teacher and counselor, told me this is something I would do. Sharing these stories is a very important part of my purpose because the spiritual aspects of the grief experience—which are essential to healing—are usually overlooked. Five years ago—and even one year ago—I wasn't ready because I still had too much to heal. Finally, I've grown enough that I can fulfill this bigger part of my spiritual mission. Now is the time!

A Penny From Africa

Lately, Ann and I have both felt inspired to expand our work to Africa. There are thousands of children there dying of starvation or AIDS, and we know that through Compassionate Passages, we can offer great solace to their suffering families. Naturally, we want to follow our inspiration, but going to Africa seems much too big a dream to even contemplate.

Strangely, despite our doubts, Ann and I both keep getting signs about Africa—being attracted to African art, noticing African music playing on the radio, and even receiving an African postcard. We're trying to piece it all together and follow the call of Spirit.

One day, before going out of town on a business trip, I was doing all the usual last-minute errands, like going to the bank and running to the post office. While walking along I found a shiny, new penny in my path. It seemed smaller than usual, and I remember thinking as I put it in my pocket that it must be foreign. Later that afternoon, I looked at the newfound penny. It certainly was foreign—in fact, it had the word "Afrika" in raised letters around the edge! I burst out crying and immediately called Ann, shouting, "You won't believe this! Dylan sent us a confirmation about working in Africa! It's a sign! I know it is! There is no logical explanation for an African penny showing up on Franklin Street in Chapel Hill, North Carolina."

I believe that African penny was Dylan saying, "Follow your dreams, Mom. Dream big and follow the signs to Africa!" Amazingly, within a year, the organizers of an African conference invited Ann and me to present our work on caring for critically ill children. Thank you, Dylan!

Points to Ponder

In this story, Dylan sends powerful medicine to his grieving mother when he delivers his words of wisdom through a spiritual medium. He is a healer for Beth—just like the spirit babies at Pachatusan are healers for the Inca people. Dylan tells his mother they had a pre-birth agreement to go through the experience of infant death together and that he was providing protection for her during the entire journey. Beth opens her mind and her heart to these profound, new ideas, thus allowing her spirit son to be the catalyst for her spiritual awakening. Beth eventually discovers her spiritual purpose is to tell her story to the world so others can awaken and understand that the death of every beloved infant has a significant spiritual purpose.

I invite you to look closely at your own life and the lessons you're learning on your journey through grief after the death of your beloved infant. Like Dylan, your spirit baby is a powerful healer who is always guiding and inspiring you to heal your grief, awaken to Spirit, and evolve to higher and higher levels of consciousness. My hope is that Beth and Dylan's story will assist you to open your soul eyes and see the spiritual purpose of your baby's death. Then you will discover your unique answers to these universal questions: "Why, God? Why did this happen to me?"

CHAPTER EIGHT

A Journey Planned by Spirit

Jacob's transition is a design of Spirit.
As Jacob's parents you are meant to be
the ones to help other people through
the experience of losing an infant.
You will be some of the leaders in this field.
—Dannion Brinkley, Psychic and Author

It was a time of great anguish for Peter and Jenny when Jacob, their beloved baby, made his transition one week after his due date. Tragically, the amniotic fluid went below the safety zone, and he strangled on the umbilical cord while still in the womb. The doctors could give no medical reason for the sudden loss of fluids; they said it was just a fluke. Jacob was stillborn and did not even take one breath.

Even before their precious child was conceived, both parents were spiritually awake and well along their individual spiritual paths. Although this did not protect them from the deep heartache all parents experience when their baby dies, it did allow Peter and Jenny to immediately view the death of their infant with both human eyes and soul eyes. Because of this dual perspective, it was much easier for them to heal their grief and come to peace in their hearts. Indeed, their healing journey has been very different from that of most parents who have lost a baby.

Enlightened Parents

Peter was born and raised on a farm in Kansas, but he was never really a farm boy; in fact, he describes himself as a fish out of water while living there. He always knew he was different from other people.

Peter became interested in energy healing as a teenager when his aunt Regina cured herself of leukemia using macrobiotics, visualizations, positive thinking, and spiritual healing. Being a pragmatist, she easily blended the physical and the spiritual aspects of life. Aunt Regina was truly Peter's first spiritual mentor, and he was very close to her.

Like his aunt, Peter combines the spiritual and the physical aspects of life. A certified massage therapist, a licensed EMT, and a Tai Chi instructor at a charter school, Peter has been practicing and teaching martial arts for over thirty years. One of the goals of this ancient art form is to become aware of the chi (spiritual energy or life force that flows through our bodies) and use it to become stronger in the physical world. Peter's daily practice of Tai Chi opened the door for him to develop a deep connection with Spirit, a connection that was in place many years before Jacob was conceived.

Jenny, like Peter, was also very connected to Spirit before her son's conception. As a child she was unaware that she was blessed with natural intuitive gifts. But as a teenager, she had a dramatic spiritual experience when her friend Tammy was killed in an automobile accident. The next day, Jenny drove to the scene and sat in her car sobbing as she viewed the site where her friend died. Looking in the rearview mirror, Jenny got the shock of her life—she could see her friend sitting in the back seat! Jenny said, "It was such a surprise. She was whole again! I didn't get any words, but I was greatly relieved to see her. It changed my whole view of death."

As a young adult, Jenny enhanced her connection to Spirit with twelve years of Tai Chi and yoga classes. Then, while training to become a massage therapist, she learned additional mind-body-spirit techniques. Given Jenny's history, it is no surprise that this young mother was quite sensitive to the higher vibrations of spiritual energy long before Jacob came into her womb. As she unconsciously moved along her path of spiritual evolution, Jenny had no clue Spirit was preparing her for a much greater purpose.

He's Here Right Now

Jenny was very connected to Jacob's spirit from the moment she knew she was pregnant. Using her well-honed intuitive abilities, Jenny developed a relationship with her son while he was in the womb.

For six months I prayed every morning and every evening for a spirit to come and bless our family. I asked for somebody powerful and loving to come be with us. We were so joyful when we knew we were pregnant! We felt absolutely blessed.

The minute Jacob came inside me, I was never alone and have never felt alone since. Early in the pregnancy, I joined a prenatal yoga class. The end of each session was a time of quiet meditation when I could completely focus on my connection with Jacob. It was a time of just "being"—we didn't have to "do" anything.

At six months, I could feel Jacob's spirit coming in and going out of his little body inside me. I'm very sensitive to spiritual energy, so I could feel his energetic presence, and I would think, "He's here right now," or "He's not here right now." This didn't scare me because it's typical for the spirit to come and go while the baby is in utero.

Jacob had so much personality in the womb. He interacted in distinct ways with each person who touched my belly. He actually had relationships while he was still inside me! When our nine-year-old Kylie would put her hand on my belly and read stories to Jacob, he would move around and kick a lot. When Rachael, age fourteen, talked to him, he was always very quiet.

Jacob Prepared Me Completely

Throughout her pregnancy, Jenny had a foreboding that Jacob would be leaving early, but she kept dismissing this idea.

I seemed to have had an inner knowing that this baby wasn't going to make it; but, of course, I denied it completely because it was too painful to contemplate.

For the first twelve weeks I was constantly wondering if Jacob was going to stay. Even after the first trimester, I wondered, "Is this for sure?" After every prenatal visit, I wrote in my journal, "He's got a heartbeat, and he's breathing. I'm really excited. He's strong. He's healthy. He's staying." I had to repeat these statements to myself between visits to keep my anxiety in check.

Even though I wrote these affirmations, I couldn't see a baby in the crib when I looked into the future; the vision just would not come. Of course, this was very disturbing, but I decided not to share it with anyone because I didn't want to make it come true. Talking about it would have given more energy to this outcome, and I didn't want to do that.

Our family is very connected; I can feel things, and I just know things. Three days before Jacob left us, I was extremely anxious about our baby. I cried out frantically to Peter, "You can't go to work today. Don't leave me! Don't leave me!" I didn't want to go to the hospital, but I didn't want him to go to work. Looking back, a part of me knew what was coming, and I was already in a panic.

My father also had a premonition the day before the tragedy occurred. He was at work that afternoon and felt a terrible darkness. He knew it was about the baby, so he just had to come and see us. He left work early and came by the house, but we weren't home. When we talked on the phone later, I assured him everything was okay. I had just been to the doctor's office for a check-up, and Jacob's heartbeat was perfect. Everything was fine.

Later that evening, I felt Jacob's spirit leave. This was nothing unusual because he was in and out a lot. I wasn't alarmed because I thought he was coming back. The next morning, I rubbed his little foot protruding from my side—I had always rubbed his little heel when I wanted his attention. He would usually respond by kicking or moving around. This time, there was no response, so I assumed he was sleeping—his body felt like a log in my belly.

An ultrasound had been previously scheduled for that morning. At the appointment, the doctor showed us a dark, black area on the ultrasound screen, where we should have been able to see Jacob's heart beating. There was nothing. We could no longer deny the reality of what was happening; we had to admit that our precious baby was already gone.

Hearing the news that Jacob was gone was a great shock, and yet at the same time, it wasn't even a surprise. From the very beginning of the pregnancy, I unconsciously knew that this was going to happen. I believe Jacob prepared me completely—his spirit was guiding me the whole way.

A Design of Spirit

Knowing intuitively that a tragedy is going to happen does not take away the human pain as the events unfold. So even though Jacob had warned Jenny, the devastating news of his death pierced her heart to the core. Then, as is the case with many stillbirths, the doctors informed Peter and Jenny that she would still have to go through labor and delivery to release Jacob's body. It was a very dark time for these parents.

Together Peter and Jenny immediately phoned family and friends, asking for support and prayers not only for Jacob's spirit, but for their own healing as well. Peter even sent an e-mail request for prayers to their spiritual community. This request quickly became part of an electronic prayer chain that went out nationally, and a deluge of prayers and assistance arrived within hours—including a most surprising visit from their spiritual mentor Dannion Brinkley.

Years before Jacob was conceived, Jenny and Peter had trained with Dannion. A spiritual teacher and author whose first book *Saved by the Light* was an international best seller, Dannion awakened to Spirit after being struck by lightening and having a near-death experience. As part of his spiritual purpose, he created an organization called Compassion in Action, which trains volunteers to be with people as they make their transition; his mission is that no one ever dies alone. Peter and Jenny felt drawn to study with Dannion; it was one of those times they simply followed their hearts.

When the doctors discovered Jacob had no heartbeat, Dannion just happened to be in town teaching at a spiritual conference. While Jenny was in the middle stages of labor, Dannion arrived at the hospital to offer his love and support. Viewing the situation with soul eyes, Dannion gifted Peter and Jenny with these words of wisdom:

> *Jacob's transition is a design of Spirit. As Jacob's parents you are meant to be the ones to help other people through the experience of losing an infant. You will be some of the leaders in this field.*

These distraught parents felt immensely blessed by Dannion's presence and his message. In our interview, Peter said:

> *Dannion brought everyone's heart light up ten to twelve notches, and our level of spiritual understanding rose equally as much. Dannion was also a huge help for Jenny's dad, who was having a very hard time; Dannion just hugged Dad and let him sob. I'd never before seen him cry like that.*

Dannion's presence at the hospital was a blessed synchronistic event! Everyone was in the right place at the right time by divine appointment. Dannion's spiritual assignment, if you will, was to remind Peter and Jenny to see the bigger picture (the spiritual journey), and view the whole situation through soul eyes.

I Am All Women

With the guidance of their spirit son, Peter and Jenny transformed the hospital birthing room into sacred space with uplifting music, prayers, and the love and support of a few close family members who were invited to be present. Both Peter and Jenny felt the presence of their spirit son and knew they were surrounded with divine love throughout labor and delivery. Jenny described her experience:

We knew Jacob's spirit had already separated from his physical form, but I still had to go through labor to deliver his lifeless body. I prayed to Jacob's spirit to help me through this process, and I had this knowing that he really was there. Our birthing room at the hospital was so peaceful that it was like being held in a soft, delicate cocoon. I felt like I was being loved through the whole experience. I know that was Jacob's doing—he created the peace and the love.

We set the mood by keeping the lights dim and playing George Winston's CD entitled Forest. *The music was sometimes powerful and sometimes soothing. It always seemed exactly right in the moment—I guess you could call it divine timing. The nurses were all wonderful, and each one contributed something special at different times during the twenty-six hours of labor. I know Jacob was helping them as they worked with me. He also helped me with the delivery—I only had to push for fifteen minutes.*

At some point during my labor, this wonderful experience unfolded. I became part of every woman who had ever given birth. I could feel myself becoming one with each of them. They all came flowing through my consciousness, and I was absolutely flooded with all their emotions. I tapped into all their fears, grief, agony, excitement, joy, and eternal love for their babies. All their emotions washed over me and through me. Spirit gave me a vision of two or three faces, but mostly it was all feelings. I will never forget the miracle of deep connection with all women. I call it being in the Oneness.

At the end of this divine experience, Spirit gave me a vision of a little girl with long brown hair running with me through these beautiful meadows on the other side. This striking child looked to be about two or three years old. I saw her face very clearly, and I just knew this spirit would be part of our family some day.

At the very moment Jacob's body was delivered, I looked to the left and saw a big, soft, orange, glowing light hovering near my bed. It was oblong in shape and about three feet across the longest part. At the time, this light brought me such comfort, but I didn't really understand how this could be.

The vision of that glowing orange light has stayed in my mind forever. Two years after this experience I asked for some clarification while in a workshop with Doreen Virtue, Ph.D. This psychologist who teaches about healing with the angels explained, "That orange light was Vadkiel, the Angel of Compassion." The message on Doreen's angel card for Vadkiel is: "Soften your heart with respect to the situation, and all the people involved, including yourself."

No wonder I felt such comfort from that orange light! I have Vadkiel's message on a magnet on my refrigerator for everybody to see. I use it whenever I'm in a tough situation. It's a great message for me because I'm usually very hard on myself.

This experience of being in Oneness with all birthing mothers as she delivered Jacob's body was very healing for Jenny. The magnificent beauty of it is imprinted on her mind and heart forever. Focusing on that sacred experience and the feelings of pure love, joy, and the bliss of Oneness continues to heal her. The simple act of remembering is always uplifting and automatically raises Jenny's vibration.

Honoring Jacob's Spirit

While holding his son's lifeless body in the delivery room, Peter felt inspired to create a spiritual blessing. He described how this sacred ceremony allowed him to shift his consciousness and come to a place of deep acceptance about his son's short time on earth.

I tell all my Tai Chi students, "The knock of Spirit offers opportunity for soul growth. There's pain in being born, and there's pain in dying. Our job is to use the pain to transform ourselves and then transcend the pain."

Initially I couldn't accept my son's death—it seemed like Spirit was asking too much of me. I had to expand my consciousness before I could transcend my pain. I guess you could say my soul growth was getting to acceptance of Jacob's death. This unfolded in a very beautiful way.

Jenny and I were alone with Jacob after the delivery, and I felt moved to do a blessing for our son. The inspiration came from a scene in the movie The Passion. *Using the words of Jesus, I opened his right eye and said, "I make all things perfect." Then I opened his left eye and said, "I make all things new." Then I made the*

149

sign of the cross on his forehead and his heart. As I opened his eyes, I could feel his spirit—it was still present with the body. In that moment, I was in touch with Jacob's soul. It's a magnificent moment of connection that will be forever in my heart.

As I finished this blessing, I felt a great expansion in my heart, and a sense of peace flowed in to replace the pain. My soul eyes opened and from this perspective, I found myself in harmony with Jacob's heavenly plan to leave this earth. I came to a place of acceptance without having to think about it; you might say acceptance came on the wings of grace.

This ritual was very grounding for me, and I felt centered once again. Before the ritual, my mind was saying, "I can't see the purpose of this tragedy." After centering, I began thinking, "We are all here for a very short time. We are all just traveling through. It doesn't matter if we are here for three months, nine months, a year, twenty years, or eighty years. It's all a very short time."

After the loss of a loved one, most people grieve the body instead of honoring the spirit. My intention is to keep my focus on honoring Jacob's spirit. This ritual was one way, and our memorial service for Jacob was another way of accomplishing this. We called his service "In Celebration of Jacob," and we did indeed celebrate his powerful spirit.

The ceremony was filled with uplifting music and readings that touched people's hearts. A woman friend who teaches with me said, "The service was so beautiful and so powerful. You were comforting all of us." People were so moved they skipped the dinner after the service saying, "I have to go home and be with my kids."

He's Just Always Here

Both Peter and Jenny live in continual connection with Jacob's powerful spirit. Peter described the ongoing interaction he has with his spirit son.

Grief thins the veil, and this is true for Jacob and me. Actually, the veil between us is very thin. His presence constantly envelops me—he's just always here. I'm busy with people all day long, so I don't interact with Jacob during the day; however, we talk at night during the quiet time before going to sleep.

Jenny also described her daily conversations with her spirit son, a source of great healing for her grief.

Because I can feel Jacob's presence all the time, I talk to him in my mind as I go about my day. "Can you believe that? Can you help me with this? Can you give me some guidance about this problem?" The answers come through inspiration as opposed to actual words. All of a sudden, the ideas will flow in, and I'll know exactly what to do. Then I just say, "Thanks, Jacob!"

Whenever I ask Jacob for something, I get a response. One afternoon while driving, I could feel Jacob's presence in the car, but I still wanted something more—something physical. Just as I had that thought, Jacob put his arms around me from behind and gave me a big hug. Imagine a little boy standing behind the driver's seat hugging his mother, who is driving. That's what it was like. It was such a loving experience! Believe me, I'll never forget that day. It was an exquisite moment of sharing pure love with my spirit son! I love our connection!

A Spicy-Sweet Smell

As human beings, we experience the world around us through our ordinary, human senses of sight, hearing, touch, taste, and smell. Not surprisingly, we have all the same senses with which to experience the spirit world; however, we have to raise our vibration in order to see something with spiritual vision, hear sounds or words with our spiritual hearing, or even smell a certain scent using our spiritual olfactory sense. People who operate at a high vibration often sense something in the spirit world while others around them miss the experience completely. Being a sensitive, Jenny is often aware of Jacob's "energetic scent."

Sometimes I can actually smell Jacob. There are no words to accurately describe the scent. It's sweet yet spicy—like nothing I've ever smelled before. It might be stronger one time and lighter another time, but it's always the same scent.

One day, my sister and I were walking around an art fair when Jacob's scent became very strong and stayed around me for a long time. I even asked my sister to come close to me so she could experience what I'd been talking about. She could feel Jacob's presence, but she couldn't smell a thing. So I had her come even closer, so she was nose-to-nose with me. Even under my own nose, where the scent was so fragrant, she could smell nothing! I was still inhaling his sweet scent with every breath; it was so real and intense that I was surprised she wasn't aware of it!

Fortunately, I know it's not just my mind playing tricks on me; he is here with me in those moments! It is an additional blessing—I treasure this spicy-sweet hint of his presence because it lights up my heart. I think of him with every breath, and I smile!

Peter added these comments about his own encounter with Jacob's scent:

I also smelled Jacob one time. I walked up to Jen to give her a hug, and this smell was so strong it actually pushed me back. It was shocking! Jen had been telling me about smelling Jacob, but I had no idea what she meant until that moment. Wow, what a powerful signal that he is right here with us!

Jacob Is My Guardian Angel

The Incas in Peru believe the spirit babies at the sacred mountain of Pachatusan are very special beings who provide potent medicine for their people. Likewise, Jenny views her spirit son, Jacob, as a powerful soul who protects her.

During the pregnancy I focused on knowing Jacob as a spirit. I was connected with his consciousness the whole time. Communicating with Jacob in the womb prepared me to keep a spiritual relationship with our baby after his transition. The relationship I had with him in the womb has continued except now his spirit is in heaven. He and I have this incredible love connection, and I can feel him with me all the time. We still have this deep, heart-to-heart love bond— not even death can break it.

Jacob no longer has a physical body, and his spirit flows easily back and forth between the two worlds. It's such a blessing that I'm aware enough to know when he comes and goes. Sometimes I think he might be in both places at the same time. I'm beginning to understand that this is possible; in fact, I've been told he can be in many places at the same time.

I have never thought of Jacob as a baby; he's the brightest light, and I think of him as a big, powerful spirit. Even while pregnant, I felt invincible because Jacob was part of me, acting as my guardian angel or protector. I knew anything could happen, and I'd be okay. To this day, I feel safe because Jacob's spirit is always around me.

Grandpa Mike: My Jacob Dreams

Grandpa Mike, Jenny's father, also has a very strong connection with Jacob's spirit. A big teddy bear of a man with a great heart, he literally radiates kindness. Mike was so looking forward to having another grandson, and he was beside himself with grief when Peter and Jenny called to say their long-awaited baby had no heartbeat.

Both Mike and his wife, Karen, live near Jenny and Peter and were very connected to Jacob throughout the pregnancy. They were present with Jenny during the labor and came back into the delivery room to hold Jacob's body immediately after the birth. Mike broke down sobbing so hard he couldn't talk; he wept from the very depths of his soul.

Mike is naturally very sensitive and became more aware of the high frequency energies of Spirit after taking Tai Chi classes from Peter.

I'm a very positive kind of person. Every day is a good day for me. This one particular day at work felt like a gray day; you know, one of those cold, winter days in the Midwest. I just had a bad feeling, and I knew it was about Jacob.

"Somebody" directed me to go over to Jenny's house, so that's what I did. When I got there, nobody was home, which worried me even more. A short time later, Jenny called to say she had just returned from the doctor's office, and Jacob was just fine. So I thought I must be nuts for having this feeling. Sadly, my premonition came true the next morning, when they discovered Jacob had no heartbeat. That was one time I didn't want to be right!

I have many days when Jacob's spirit is with me. I'll be at the house working on a project or in the garden when I get that feeling that Jacob sends me. It's a warm, cozy feeling that just flows right through me. Whenever it comes, I know Jacob is close by.

Feeling Jacob's presence brings me great comfort. At those times, I find myself thinking, "I know where he is. He knows who I am, and he wants to be with me." Then I sigh with a deep sense of peace.

When Jenny was pregnant, we knew it was a boy, and I kept thinking, "Here's another grandson to golf with me." I never got to take Jacob out on a golf course, but we do many things in my dreams. When I'm sleeping, Jacob and I do all the usual family things—he's just like my other two grandsons. We play baseball together and go golfing; I enjoy every minute of it, even if it's only in my dreams.

Whenever I have one of my Jacob dreams, I wake up with that warm, cozy feeling in my heart and a big smile on my face. He's a wonderful grandson, and I love his spirit dearly!

Here we see that Jacob is a heart healer for his grandfather. He comes in dreams to meet the emotional needs of his beloved Grandpa Mike. After these dream visits, Mike feels the peace of spiritual love and connection in his heart.

Sister Kylie: I'm Not Afraid Anymore

Kylie, Jacob's sister, who was nine years old when he made his transition, talked to him in the womb and started a relationship with him then. Like Grandpa Mike, Kylie is very aware of Jacob's spirit and continues to have many encounters with him.

I'll be sitting at the kitchen table just thinking, and I'll see Jacob right on the table in front of me. He looks like a little baby; in fact, he looks just like his pictures. The first time I saw him, I was really scared. Then, after it kept happening, I wasn't so scared. Now, I feel happy when I see him. I wonder why he visits me. I don't get any answers about that.

My hamster died a few months ago, and we were having a little funeral for him in the family room. Jacob showed up right by the fireplace! I was so surprised! I thought it was cool that he wanted to attend.

Before, I was real scared about things like ghosts, but because I've seen Jacob as a spirit baby, I'm not afraid anymore. I don't tell any of my friends about Jacob's spirit—they don't want to know. I think it scares them. Also, I used to be scared about dying, but I'm not anymore.

One day, I came home from school and decided to make a drawing about Jacob. I drew a little ghost up in the right-hand corner and a tombstone in the middle of the paper. Then I wrote this message:

"Jacob Markus, my brother,

I wish your body was still with me."

I put "R.I.P. 2004-2004" on the tombstone; then I wrote this beside the tombstone:

"Died 11-6-04 ~ Born 11-7-04

Rest your body, live on with your soul.

Even though your body isn't here with us,

Your spirit still lives on inside."

I put the drawing on the front door so Mom would see it when she came home. She got so excited when she saw it! While she was driving around doing errands, she asked Jacob to give her something physical to hang onto. I guess I got the message and did it for him! Mom sure loves that drawing!

Here we see Jacob being a teacher-healer for his sister. He helped Kylie alleviate her dread of ghosts and her fear of death, which are major changes in beliefs about the nature of the afterlife. In addition, Jacob inspired Kylie, and together they created a poetic picture-message for their mom.

The Track and the Trail

Although Peter and Jenny were devastated when they first discovered their baby had no heartbeat, their spiritual view of life helped them see the situation with both human eyes and soul eyes. Before Jacob came into his life, Peter had studied spiritual teachings from different cultures, including the Toltec wisdom traditions that originated in southern Mexico thousands of years ago. One of their teachings became significant for Peter after Jacob's transition.

There's a story about the track and the trail in the ancient Toltec tradition. The track is the life journey you have planned for yourself with your conscious mind; the trail is the journey planned by Spirit. The Toltecs teach that the "knock of Spirit" can shove you off your track; then you find yourself on the trail.

We made a conscious choice to have another baby, but Spirit knocked us off our track when Jacob died. Now, we are following a trail, and we get little glimpses of where it is leading us. Others, like Dannion, who are spiritually awake, keep giving us messages about where the trail is leading.

After Jacob's death, I remembered one of my Kabala teachers saying that evolved spiritual beings stay here on earth only as long as they have to. Jenny and I both understand that Jacob is a very evolved soul.

Heavenly wisdom and earthly wisdom are very different; heavenly wisdom holds an eternal picture, while earthly wisdom does not. Jacob had a heavenly reason for his short life here and in just two months, we are gradually coming to understand bits and pieces of that reason.

Like Peter, Jenny rather quickly came to accept that Jacob's short time here on earth was planned at the soul level. This understanding allowed Jenny to heal much of her heartache within months of Jacob's transition.

Dannion said, "Jacob's transition is a design of Spirit." This idea has helped me so much. I've come to understand that I'm not the only one creating my life—Jacob is part of the design, and so is Spirit. I used to think everything was up to me; I believed I could decide things and have some control by planning out my life. One of the lessons of Jacob's death is that we are not in control. There's a Spirit design at work here that Peter and I would never have consciously chosen.

I had some subtle clues about this Spirit design at various stages of the pregnancy. Because I was aware of them, I felt responsible for everyone's grief. I've been able to shift out of that belief. It's only been a few months now since Jacob's transition, and at this point in my grief journey, I believe this was a soul agreement between all three of us—Peter, Jacob, and me. When I think of it this way, I understand it's not my fault.

A New Purpose for Jenny

For a full year after Jacob's transition, Jenny focused time and energy on healing her grief and then awakened to a new spiritual purpose. Even though she was already spiritually awake, it was a time of deep soul growth for this young mother.

During this time I've done so much to heal my grief. I've had this deep need to read a lot of spiritual books. My favorites are: Angelic Presence *by Cammie Lammert and Sue Friedeck,* Life Touches Life *by Lorraine Ash, and* We Were Gonna Have a Baby, But We Had an Angel Instead *by Pat Schwiebert.*

Also, I've released a lot of tears, and I've talked about Jacob any chance I got. Most people give me really strange looks when they hear me talking about my son as a spirit. I guess they're not used to a grieving mother talking about communicating with her spirit baby.

There have been some major changes for me since going through this experience with Jacob. Now I have a direct connection to heaven through Jacob; consequently, my intuitive gifts have become much stronger. I am constantly aware of being in my body here on earth while at the same time tuning into Jacob's world and communicating with his spirit.

I remember my dreams more frequently, and they are much more intense. All my senses are heightened in my dreams—I can actually feel myself touching other people. I also have less attachment to worldly things. This just happened without my thinking about it.

One of the biggest changes is that my fear of death simply vanished. In fact, when Jacob first left, Peter asked me what I was feeling. I told him, "I'm ready to go be with Jacob. He's the one I talk to all the time. He's the light of my life." Now, that feeling has passed, and I know I have a spiritual purpose here to fulfill, so I'm staying. My mission is to assist others as they transition. I'm also here to help others heal from their grief experience.

Within months of Jacob's transition, I started volunteering in the NICU at our local hospital. My arms needed to be wrapped around a baby! It was the hardest thing I could do, but it helped me heal. I could feel Jacob's spirit right there with me as I rocked these babies. He helped me have the strength to keep my heart open to these very sick little ones and their families.

I also returned to massage therapy work with the residents of an elder care facility. After Jacob's transition, numerous women "came out to me" and told me their stories of losing a baby forty, fifty, or sixty years before. Most had never talked about their baby and were still filled with grief after all these years. One woman named Maxine was still grieving as if her baby had died yesterday. We talked a lot and she really healed as she cried on my massage table. Strangely, as they were healing, I was healing. It seemed so easy and so natural to be doing this grief work—I know it was all part of the plan that Dannion predicted. God sent me to do this work with the older generation.

Two Years Later

The second year after Jacob's death Peter and Jenny found themselves dealing with a great deal of relationship stress. They both knew that it's very common for many couples to have relationship problems and to even divorce after the death of a child. However, this knowledge did not protect them from having the same experience.

Of course, we had heard that many couples have difficulties after the death of a child. But, we didn't know it was going to happen to us. It was such a shock!

At times, Peter blamed himself for Jacob's death; at other times, he blamed me for forcing the pregnancy when we weren't totally ready. We had numerous goals we wanted to complete before having a baby. None of these were complete when we conceived Jacob. So we didn't have everything ready at the human level.

When I looked at our situation with human eyes, I definitely blamed myself for Jacob's death. I would say to myself, "I should have known not to let the pregnancy go past his due date. I should have listened to my intuitive knowing that he was going to leave and done something to stop it."

Having a baby die can definitely make or break a relationship. We never felt like we were going to divorce, but we had some very tough times. We both had to have the courage to express our blaming thoughts, listen to each other with deep understanding, and move through it with a loving heart. Thankfully, our strong love for each other kept us going. After many months of dealing with the blame issues openly, we came to this understanding: We are not responsible for Jacob's death. Jacob was supposed to be here at the exact time that he came into my womb. We were meant to feel the devastating grief, live through it, and grow from the experience. It was all meant to be.

A Granddaughter Arrives

Two years after Jacob's transition, Jenny's stepdaughter announced she was pregnant. Peter and Jenny intended to have another baby, but they weren't ready yet. Consequently, this announcement generated many mixed feelings for Jenny.

It was a very confusing time for me—I was happy for my step-daughter, but at the same time, unhappy for myself. Initially I felt really hurt because she was having a baby before we did. Thankfully, I was able to resolve these feelings fairly quickly and open my heart to this new being. The whole family was so excited about this baby who was coming to join our family.

While doing a pregnancy massage for my stepdaughter, I was given a vision of a little girl about two or three years old. She came to me so clearly! I was quite shocked to see that it was the same little girl who had appeared in my Oneness experience. This little girl had the exact same face. I thought to myself, "She's here!"

At her birth, I looked closely at my granddaughter Essa—she had the exact face shown to me by Spirit in both my visions. Then I held her to my heart and blessed her for coming to our family as my granddaughter.

Pregnant Again

Jenny discovered she was pregnant the same weekend little Essa was born. It was a little more than three years after Jacob was conceived. Peter and Jenny did not announce their news at the time, because they wanted the whole family to stay focused on the arrival of the new granddaughter. Jenny described her feelings about this pregnancy.

It was a conscious decision to conceive, and Peter and I both felt ready. Actually, we were thrilled to be bringing another baby into our home. We were ecstatic!

We soon discovered this baby was a boy, and we named him Marcus. My pregnancy with Marcus was totally different from my first pregnancy. The whole experience with Jacob was such a spiritual thing; I had my head in the clouds the whole time and had absolutely no physical discomfort—in fact, I was rarely aware of the physical aspects of the experience. With Marcus, on the other hand, I was very much here in the physical world. I had all-day sickness, which was so horrible. This time I was very grounded and kept my focus on the practical aspects of the pregnancy.

I had such a spiritual connection with Jacob in the womb, but I just didn't want to feel that connection with Marcus. There was so much pain involved when Jacob left that I just couldn't go there again. I felt there would be less heartache for me if something happened to this baby, so I chose not to connect. I wasn't giving him the opportunity to break my heart.

Of course I felt terribly guilty about this decision. I poured my heart out to my cousin Cathy, who had also lost a baby at birth and then had a successful second pregnancy. I told her, "I'm not connecting with this baby. I can't. I don't want to." She responded,

"That's okay. You will at some time. You'll know when that time comes." Strangely, everything shifted after she gave me permission to not connect and not feel guilty about it. Only then could I allow my heart to open to this beautiful, new being in my womb. It was about the third month of the pregnancy when I bonded with our new baby.

Marcus taught me to live every day in the present. I had to stay focused on right now without looking into the future or giving my attention to the past. This was the only way I could handle all my horrific, ever-present fears. I knew there was no guarantee that we wouldn't have to go through the death of another baby. Peter agreed saying, "That's right. There's no free pass."

I didn't release all my human pain about Jacob until after Marcus was born. After Jacob's transition, my mom and I talked about him all the time. Early on, she spoke of the look on my face when I delivered Jacob. I didn't know what she meant at the time; however I could never ask her to describe that look. After Marcus was home safe with us, I finally had the courage to ask. She answered, "I saw a tremendous amount of sorrow." I cried deeply, yet once again, the great sorrow of it all piercing my heart. Eventually, my tears stopped flowing, and I slipped into a state of peace; that's when I somehow knew I was finally finished with the heavy grief about Jacob.

As I look back, I see that I've been in a holding pattern for three and a half years. There seemed to be a bubble around me and I was stuck inside of it. I couldn't lose any weight; it seemed my body wasn't ready to let go of anything. Everything about my life felt heavy and stuck. Even my conversations were focused on death and grief.

After Marcus was born everything shifted. The extra weight from both pregnancies seemed to fall away effortlessly. I feel so much lighter both mentally and emotionally. The sorrow is gone from my face, and the sadness in my eyes is replaced with a shining light. My whole being is filled with a brightness I couldn't allow before I knew Marcus was here to stay. Marcus is such a gift to our family. He has healed a lot of hearts!

When we look at Marcus, we see Jacob—they look enough alike to be twins. In fact, we really think of them as twins. Jacob is right here with Marcus and me. Marcus is our earthly child and Jacob

*is our heavenly child. We didn't lose him—he's right here with us
every minute of the day and night. When we look in our hearts, he's
everywhere.*

Points to Ponder

Jenny and Peter are both very conscious of themselves as spiritual beings
before Jacob is conceived, so even before conception, it is easy and natural
for them to honor their precious infant as a spiritual being. They see the
whole experience of Jacob's birth and death with both human eyes and
soul eyes, and are thus able to balance their human grief with spiritual
joy and love. *Can you expand your ideas about your infant who stayed
only a short time here on earth? Can you see him or her as a powerful
spiritual being instead of a helpless little baby? It will be easier for you to
transform your grief into peace, joy, and love when you do so.*

Once again, this story illustrates that whenever an infant dies, there is a
sacred pre-birth plan developed at the soul level for both the death of this
infant and the spiritual evolution of the family as they heal their grief.
Within hours of hearing that Jacob has no heartbeat, their spiritual teacher,
Dannion Brinkley, arrives on the scene to remind Peter and Jenny of this
agreement. As Peter and Jenny embrace Dannion's message, they create a
new model for healing grief. Teaching others to find a spiritual solution to
the tragedy of infant loss is obviously part of their soul mission.

In this story, Jenny, Peter, and Jacob illustrate that, in our modern American
culture, we each have the potential to deal with grief like the ancient Inca
people. Jacob's spirit acts as a healer for his parents, his grandfather, his
sister, and everyone connected to his grieving family. Indeed, Jacob brings
powerful medicine for all.

CHAPTER NINE

⁓꩜⁓

The Bliss of Oneness

*Lucas has a Buddha-like energy—his presence inspires
deep transformation and healing. His spirit is pure love,
and his energetic presence invites people into
that same state. I believe this is his purpose.*
—Craig, Lucas' Father

Craig and his wife, Liesel, awaited the birth of their precious baby boy
with such joy and excitement. Their deep heart connections with this
soul they named Lucas began even before conception. They loved him
from that day in a beautiful mountain meadow near their home in Santa
Barbara, California, when they felt his spirit asking to join their family,
and their love grew stronger each month while he developed in the womb.
For the entire nine months, they were blissfully unaware that, in the end,
they would retain their spiritual bond with this beloved soul, but not their
physical connection.

It's been four years since Lucas came to earth and made his transition several
days later, so it's not surprising that his parents are still on their individual
healing journeys. Because both Craig and Liesel were spiritually awake
long before their baby's conception, birth, and death, they had the ability
to see these blessed events with soul eyes. As Craig tells their inspiring
story, he paints a sacred picture of death from the soul's perspective—
including the wonder, the joy, and the bliss of sharing eternal love with
their beloved infant immediately after his transition. It's a wondrous story
that will touch your heart and uplift your soul.

Being Led by Spirit

Craig, a sensitive man with the heart and soul of an artist, has a talent for
singing and playing the guitar, and had always dreamed of making his
living through his music. A man of great determination, he struggled in this
endeavor until he was thirty-two; however, it seems Spirit had a greater
plan for him. Over time this greater plan filtered into his consciousness,

and he shifted his focus to another passion that had been evolving slowly for a number of years—to work as a healer.

Craig described his journey of being led by Spirit to discover this facet of his soul purpose. At age twenty-five, he felt inspired to go to massage school, his first introduction to Eastern practices like Tai Chi and Qi Gong. He enjoyed it at the time, but had no intention of making these healing practices his career.

Three years later, Craig started searching for a way to relieve his chronic back pain. Something deep within kept pushing him to explore yoga. Resisting for a while, he finally took classes, which he says blew his mind. One evening while doing hip stretches, he burst out crying and found himself wondering, "What is this all about?" At the time he didn't realize that yoga is a spiritual practice—he saw it only as a way to help alleviate his back pain. Attending these classes triggered a deep awakening process in Craig, and he soon found himself on a journey seeking universal truths. He began reading about Yogananda and the other mystics. During this time, he and his band were performing at a hotel, where he met Penny, a fellow employee who was also conscious of Spirit in her life. Penny and Craig had deep, ongoing conversations about life, spiritual books, and Spirit.

One day Penny said, "I don't really tell very many people this, but I'm psychic, and I see some things that might help you. You should go see my mom, Sarah; she's a Reiki Master. She could help you move some of the energy that's stuck in your body, and also help you awaken more to what you're doing."

Craig didn't have a clue about Reiki, but somehow he trusted this guidance from his new friend. He called her mother that same night and scheduled his first appointment for the next day. Craig described his first session.

Sarah was working on my hips, and energy was pouring out of me. I was just bawling the whole time as I released years of old, toxic, emotional energy. This first Reiki session was the pivotal moment of my spiritual awakening. I made a deep connection with Spirit that day and have never been the same."

Craig became Sarah's Reiki student immediately. After completing the first two levels of training, he began practicing this ancient healing art with clients. He loved every minute of sharing this spiritual energy with people, and they seemed to heal at a very deep level.

Eventually, Craig was guided to explore the age-old art of acupuncture. As with Reiki, he loved it from the first class. His passion for these two ancient modalities inspired him to create a healing practice in Santa Barbara, where he combines them to help his clients attain well-being on all levels—physical, mental, emotional, and spiritual. Individuals may come to him because of back pain, but Craig will shift the focus to releasing blocked emotional energy, the underlying cause of their physical suffering. Craig talked about his work, saying, "This deep work not only promotes healing in my clients, it feeds my soul as well. I know I'm doing what I came here to do."

Creating a Soul Family

Craig followed his intuitive guidance to create his career; likewise, he approached his personal life in the same way. As you have witnessed in other stories, souls make agreements before coming to earth as human beings, and are then guided by Spirit to find each other among millions of people in order to carry out their divine contracts. Of course, for the most part, individuals follow this plan without even being conscious that it exists. Craig explained how he and his wife connected romantically.

Liesel and I had known each other casually years earlier and reconnected at the time I began my Reiki training. On our first date, I actually gave her a session. It was a transformational moment! Before long, we began meditating together and participating in other spiritual practices. This allowed us to connect in a deep, soulful way. We soon discovered we were in love and decided to make a life together.

Although Liesel had previously been a member of several meditation groups and had experienced her own awakening, her connection to Spirit was dormant when we began dating. Our joint meditation sessions reawakened her spiritual abilities. Now my wife is a gifted intuitive healer, as well as a Reiki practitioner and teacher.

Reiki was a big part of our joint spiritual path. We spent our honeymoon at a place called The Sanctuary on the little Thai island of Ko Panang. It was really magical. There were no cars—just little boats cruising around. We stayed the whole summer and completed our Reiki Master training together. It was such a powerful trip.

Six months after their romantic honeymoon, Craig and Liesel went to India to attend a friend's wedding. They stayed on to study yoga with a venerable swami who, though not well known, carried great wisdom.

Craig thought this sage was quite something with a beard to his chest and flowing, white robes. During one of their meditation groups, they received a prophecy that Craig will never forget.

> *Without warning, the swami turned to Liesel and announced, "This child that's coming to you is going to be very pious and do great things for the planet." I had goose bumps everywhere when he made that statement. Those goose bumps were saying, "Pay attention here!" At the same time, I was thinking, "What child?"*

This prediction was quite a shock to both Craig and Liesel. They had already decided they were not having any children so they could live a carefree life, traveling the world. They spent the next four months vacillating, asking, "Should we have children? Should we not?" At the human level, they never did make a decision. Craig described what happened next on their journey.

> *We had this amazing experience. It was springtime in the mountains around Santa Barbara. It was a magical day—everything was just perfect. We were sitting in this stream, enjoying the absolute beauty, when Liesel looked at me and said, "I feel this spirit who wants to come right now. I really feel him so strong." I answered, "Yeah, I feel him too. There's a real thickness in the air around us."*

> *We looked at each other and simultaneously reached the same conclusion. "Let's bring him in." It was one of those synchronistic moments that we never could have planned. It just happened. That afternoon in the mountain meadow, we conceived our baby with intention. We both had a feeling this child would be a boy—we both felt his male energy.*

Craig and Liesel intuitively kept their soul agreement to bring this precious baby boy into the world. Notice that they didn't use their logical minds— instead, they made this decision from a deeper place, the level of heart and soul. This sacred conception is a clear example of ancient soul promises being honored.

Womb Communication

Craig and Liesel both developed a really strong bond with Lucas while he was in the womb, so he was already part of the family before his birth. Craig had a way of communicating with his son that didn't need words.

> *I sometimes put my hands on my wife's belly in order to feel our baby's energy. Each time, I thought, "Wow! This being is so*

amazingly present. He is so powerful!" I could totally feel him. His energy always felt very peaceful—like Buddha. After connecting with him in this way, I often sent him Reiki energy.

Craig and Liesel had different ways of communicating with Lucas while he was in the womb. Liesel is clairvoyant—that is, she has eyes to see what's happening beyond the range seen by others in their ordinary five-sense reality. Each time she tuned in to the baby, she'd see a prism of purple light. One day late in her pregnancy, Liesel was hanging out with her best friend, who was also pregnant with a baby boy. These two mothers were due to deliver within days of each other. As they sat talking, Liesel observed a luminous tube of light flowing between their bellies. It seemed to be a "love beam" connecting their babies.

Lucas also sent messages to Craig and Liesel through Dr. Michael, a chiropractor Liesel began seeing regularly even before she became pregnant. Also trained in acupuncture, this man is so sensitive to energy that he has been able to expand his lifework to include the roles of healer and psychic. Liesel's ongoing appointments with Dr. Michael to alleviate back pain during her pregnancy opened the door for him to become a close family friend. Craig described this interesting phenomenon.

Throughout the pregnancy, Dr. Michael would call every few weeks and say, "Your son's spirit keeps coming to me and asking me to call you and tell you stuff. He says to tell you, 'Talk to me in the womb.' You both need to focus more of your attention on him."

The Birth

Craig and Liesel planned to have a home birth assisted by two midwives and a doula. The pregnancy was completely normal; there were no distress signals—nothing to indicate the baby or mother would have any problems. Lucas had good heart tones throughout the long labor process. Then, minutes before he was born, Janet, one of the midwives, had a feeling that something wasn't right. She called 911 for an ambulance and cried out, "Get the oxygen ready." The other midwife responded, "What's going on? Why are you doing that?" Janet answered, "I just don't feel right about this birth, and I want some support."

Lucas couldn't breathe when he was born—in fact, he almost died as he was delivered. The midwives performed CPR until the paramedics arrived. Finally, Lucas took a few labored breaths but wasn't able to continue on his own. Craig and Liesel live around the corner from the fire station, so the ambulance arrived in just a couple of minutes. Lucas had to be intubated before he was put into the ambulance for the short ride to the hospital. Craig described their reaction to these traumatic events.

Liesel and I were both in shock—it all seemed surreal. At the hospital the doctors examined our baby and said, "Most of his brain cells are dead. There's no hope that he'll live without life support. It's a question of when, not if, you take him off." We could hardly believe what the doctors were telling us.

A Name Guided by Spirit

While their son was in the womb, Craig and Liesel had great difficulty choosing a name for him. They had discussed the names Lucas, which means "bringer of light," or Jai, which means "victory." However, they hadn't made a final decision and were still undecided when they arrived at the hospital. Craig described how they came to name their baby.

After getting our infant son settled in the NICU, we were ushered into his doctor's office. We looked up and saw her nameplate— there, in bold letters, was "Dr. Leuke"! We both saw this as a sign. In that moment, we decided to name our son Lucas Jai.

This confirmed an earlier message that came late in the pregnancy. One evening our housekeeper gifted us with homemade tamales for dinner. As we finished the meal, we noticed there was a picture of Luke Skywalker on the plate she'd brought. Liesel and I both thought, "He's giving us a sign with this plate. He's making the decision for us." Strangely, we still didn't come to an agreement about his name.

Making the Decision

Lucas was on life support for two days at the hospital. In spite of the doctors' dire prognosis for Lucas, Craig and Liesel hoped for a miracle. Craig described this very traumatic time.

Right from the beginning, it seemed like our son's spirit wasn't really present. He was alive, but not really alive. I say that because his eyes were vacant—there was no light present. I couldn't connect with his spirit when I looked in his eyes. Of course, we were freaked out and distraught—it was really intense.

Our thoughts were all over the place. "Should we start doing healing work with Lucas? Can we create a miracle using the combined energies of our friends who do healing work? Should we keep Lucas on life support? What kind of life would he have being brain dead? Is it better for him if we disconnect the machines?" We couldn't seem to make a decision.

The morning of the second day at the hospital, our friend Michael came walking through the door just as we were discussing our options. It was so synchronistic! We didn't call him—he just arrived at exactly the right time.

Michael said with great compassion, "I was up all night talking with Lucas. At first he was confused about whether or not to stay on earth; but he's decided he can do more work from the other side. He wants you to let him go."

A shiver went through me, and I got goose bumps everywhere. It was hard to hear those words; yet at the same time, it was a relief. Michael's message gave Liesel and me the support we needed to take Lucas off the life support machines and release his spirit.

Connecting in Oneness

The next morning, the sun was rising as Craig stood looking out the hospital window. Liesel was in her hospital bed, crying and thinking about their precious infant on life support down the hall.

Lying down next to my wife, I took her hand and said, "Let's do something instead of just sitting here in our pain. Let's see if we can connect with Lucas on the spirit level since it doesn't seem like he's in his body."

We started going into a deep meditative state. Within a few minutes, we had the same experience of seeing and feeling this amazing purple light envelop us like a huge, warm blanket. There was a diffuse white star in the center of this energy. It was like we were having a joint dream. We talked to each other as it was happening. "Do you feel that?" "Yes, I feel it." "Do you see that?" "Yes." "Do you see this?" "Yes."

Wrapped in this blanket of purple, we were lifted to a higher place. It was like Reiki energy multiplied one hundred times! We were totally immersed in the purple light of our son's energetic presence, and Liesel, Lucas, and I merged effortlessly into the field of Oneness. Strangely, my wife and I both started laughing and giggling, and we couldn't stop. I guess you could say we were in bliss!

The strangest thing happened to both of us during this experience. It was like a bomb went off and blew away our earthly reality. We were just floating; there was no hospital and no bed—we weren't even aware of our own bodies.

During the experience I thought, "I get it now. We are so much more than this body. We are infinite beings." In the moment, it seemed like Spirit was saying to us, "Okay, now, here's the real deal. Here's the truth about your existence there on earth."

I didn't hear any words or see anything other than the purple light. Lucas seemed to be conveying the message, "I'm with you. I'm right here. You don't have to be worried and tripped out with grief."

We stayed in this altered state for over an hour; by then, we were both super-charged with spiritual energy. It was such a compelling experience. It was so powerful! I thought to myself, "I don't know if I can even talk to anybody about this. They're going to expect us to be in such pain, and here we are laughing hysterically!"

Because Liesel and Craig were both healers, they had a framework on which to hang this experience. That was certainly a blessing; otherwise, they would have had a very difficult time making sense of what had happened. As the purple energy transported these devastated parents beyond their ordinary human experience, it lifted them above their grief, and their eternal souls merged with the Oneness. In this state, there is no death, so there was nothing to grieve.

A Spiritual Community

Craig and Liesel have lived in Santa Barbara for over twenty years and are part of a very supportive community. Consequently, they are surrounded by a wonderful group of long-time friends and close colleagues, many of whom are involved in the healing arts. In addition, before Lucas was born, Craig attended acupuncture school and bonded with his fellow students. Craig described how this vast support system affected both his experience at the hospital and his healing journey.

We have a group of friends we call our psychic network—they are all intuitives, psychics, and mediums. Many make their living by giving readings. Others do body work of various kinds—massage, acupuncture, chiropractic adjustments, and cranial sacral work.

There was a group of over one hundred people involved somehow in Lucas's birth and death. They continually offered their love and a variety of healing modalities to support us throughout this time with Lucas. Many seemed to be deeply affected by the experience and had their own individual healing or awakening. Lucas was the connecting force for our whole community.

A Sacred Time of Letting Go

Craig and Liesel both come from large extended families, and many of these relatives traveled from all over the country to provide support. In addition, as Craig and Liesel were getting ready to take Lucas off the machines, friends and colleagues from their healing community spontaneously arrived at the hospital. As if it were planned, fifteen or so people just showed up. Liesel and Craig decided to invite them all to participate in the ceremony.

> *I told our friends, "We're getting ready to disconnect life support and let go of Lucas. You're welcome to stay and participate, but feel free to leave." All of them stayed. All the love and support from these wonderful people really grounded the energy and created a sacred space for us. It was awesome! It seemed every person who showed up was meant to be there. To this day, it touches my heart that everyone stayed. I still cry when I tell this part of the story.*

Dr. Leuke offered the use of her office for Lucas' transition. Liesel and Craig both appreciated this kindness, especially because the room had a wall of windows and was bathed in sunlight. After the three of them met in the NICU, Dr. Leuke took Lucas off life support and gently handed him to his parents, who swaddled him in blankets and held him close. Then they carried their precious child to her office, where their friends and family were waiting in sacred silence. Craig described the scene.

> *It was a new way to experience death. Lucas was barely breathing, yet it was fifteen or twenty minutes before he actually made his transition. The whole group sang to our precious infant as he was crossing to the other side. Over and over we sang a farewell blessing used in Kundalini yoga,* The Long Time Sun. *The words were perfect.*

> *May the long time sun*
>
> *Shine upon you,*
>
> *All love surround you,*
>
> *And the pure light within you*
>
> *Guide your way on.*

> *The whole scene was heart-wrenching, yet magical and sacred. I remember thinking, "This is how I want to die. Why can't we all*

die like this?" Our culture doesn't do well with death. What we did with Lucas was a different way of connecting with death. It was so beautiful.

Celebration of Life

After Lucas' transition at the hospital, everyone spontaneously went to Craig and Liesel's home for a gathering that turned into a three-day celebration of Lucas' life. People brought food, drinks, flowers, musical instruments, and poems they had written. It was like a big open house with their spiritual community coming and staying for as long as it felt right to them. Craig described this event.

It seemed like most of our visitors were charged with Spirit and light. There was so much positive, uplifting energy piping into our house the entire time. It was awesome! We celebrated Lucas!

Another Ceremony to Honor Lucas

As part of their goodbyes, Craig and Liesel held a memorial ceremony for Lucas in the big library of the hospital. The intention was to honor Lucas, but even as they started the ceremony, they had no idea how it was going to unfold. Liesel's prenatal yoga teacher, Lili, and her devout husband, Steven, led this event with the assistance of a hospital pastor. Each of them brought a unique energy to the process.

We sat in front of a little altar the leaders prepared in the center of the room. Without speaking, the whole group formed a circle around us, sending healing energy. Everything seemed to flow with a seamless continuity that was awesome; everyone moved in sync as if directed by an invisible conductor. It was really powerful! We were surrounded by so much love. It was exquisitely beautiful and so peaceful.

People were spontaneously getting up to speak. Everyone present had a chance to share. None of it was really planned except for the few poems people brought to read. Some brought their guitars and shared a song. It seemed all of it was coming through from the divine.

After a bit, I took a friend's guitar and sang a song I'd composed for Lucas—it was one I used to sing it to him routinely while he was in the womb. I tell you, he was right there on my shoulder the whole time I was singing! I could feel his presence.

Liesel and I both received an infusion of energy and were lifted to a very high place during this gathering. We seemed to be grieving less than anyone else in the group. We had some sorrow mixed in at times, but it was not the prevalent feeling. Mostly, we were high on the spiritual energy and seemed to be floating through the experience.

My psychic friend Penny was sitting next to Liesel and me. She kept announcing, "He's here. He's here. He's all around you. He keeps saying, 'Look how beautiful my parents are.'"

There was a hummingbird flying just outside the windows during the entire ceremony. Afterwards, we looked up the meaning of hummingbird in Ted Andrew's book Animal Speak, *and found that hummingbirds represent joy. Indeed, there was a lot of joy in this ceremony.*

At some point Steven organized an African ritual. We stood in the center of the group and he placed everyone in concentric circles around us. Those in the inner circle put their hands on us, and those in the outer circles were connected to someone who was touching us. Everyone began sending divine energy to us through their hands.

Then Steven asked me to make a tone to assist our baby's spirit as he continued his journey Home. Reaching deep within, I found a strong, rich tone that flowed from me and lasted for several minutes. As I held this note, Steven directed everyone to duplicate my sound. Then everybody in the room started resonating with this tone, piping energy into us. We all toned together for about five minutes. I felt like we were blasted off into outer space. Everyone was crying and laughing at the same time. It so awesome!

The entire ceremony was really a healing event. The whole place was vibrating with the intense feelings of grief as well as deep spiritual love. So many opened their hearts to both the pain and the love. Mostly, people were not shying away from the process of experiencing the heart-wrenching pain of losing a loved one. This was so different from the norm. In our culture we're so afraid of emotional pain. We deny it or medicate it—we don't let pain be part of our existence.

My parents were both very present and very grounded. They embraced everything and accepted our way of dealing with death.

My dad is a captain who flies large jet planes—he's not one to express a lot of emotion or have deep conversations about life or death. At the end of the ceremony, Dad came up to us, looked both of us in the eye, and said, "You guys are our teachers." It was such a pivotal moment! For him to share at a level this deep was a powerful opening for our relationship.

A Giant Healing Wave

After Lucas' death, a giant healing wave went through many of the family, friends, and colleagues who attended the events for Lucas. Little miracles were happening throughout the whole group. For instance, Liesel felt her brother had always kept his distance from her. After the ceremony, he really opened his heart, held her close, and announced with tears in his eyes, "I love you." In that moment, their relationship was rekindled.

A married couple who had a one-year-old child came up to Craig in the hallway of the hospital and said: "We were about to get a divorce. After this ceremony for Lucas, we've changed our minds. We're going to make it work." It seemed the whole process of celebrating Lucas' life brought them to a higher understanding of why they had chosen one another. Four years later they are still together—and they've brought another precious child into their family.

Craig had this to say about the wave of healing.

I often wonder how this happened. During the ceremony one of our friends shed light on the whole event when she said, "Birth and death are the times when we are closest to God. Because Lucas' birth and death were so close together, it gave a lot of people access to Spirit." This makes so much sense to me. Our son's transition seemed to open up many in our spiritual community.

Deep Communion With Lucas

In the early weeks after their son's transition to the other side, Liesel and Craig had repeated experiences of deep communion with his spirit.

I'd wake up every morning and say to Liesel, "Let's connect with Lucas again." We'd lie there on our bed and get into a deep meditative state. Then Lucas would come to be with us, and we were both enveloped in his purple energy. We would both be filled with "the juice" and remain in our state of bliss. He came every morning for two weeks—it was just like clockwork.

We discovered that Sophie, one of our midwives, was having these intense experiences along with us. Lucas would visit us, and we would feel him as this blanket of energy coming in and surrounding us. It was this really thick, super-charged energy—like Reiki times ten. It was so powerful. It was also exuberant—like laughing energy and total joy. Then Sophie would call and describe the same thing happening to her. That was pretty wild.

Liesel and Craig stayed in this altered state of reality for two full weeks and were infused with spiritual energy the whole time. The blissful feeling stayed no matter what they did and amazingly, they had no grief during this time. In fact, Craig's state of bliss went on for a month.

The Grief Journey

About two weeks after his death, Lucas started pulling his energy away from his parents; they could both feel it gradually dissipate. Sadly, he was no longer so intensely present. Lucas seemed to be saying to his parents, "You need to deal with the physical reality. Constantly connecting with me is keeping you from that."

After this separation, Liesel started grieving really deeply. Craig was still floating in the bliss for another two weeks—it was a full month before he started feeling the loss. At first, it caused a bit of tension between them because Liesel was in despair, and Craig was still high on the spiritual energy. Craig explained how this imbalance turned out to be a blessing.

There was never a time in our entire grieving process that we were both grief-stricken at the same time. It was always one or the other. In a way, this was good because we were never in the total, dark depths of grief at the same time. There was a natural support system between us. One person was always strong enough to hold space and provide support for the other, who could then let go into the anguish of losing our son.

Once the grief started for Craig, it was extremely intense. There were times when he couldn't even get out of bed—it was like something had sucked all the energy out of his body, and he was left with an overwhelming heaviness. This state often lasted for days, sometimes even weeks. The best solution seemed to be getting various healing treatments like massage, cranial sacral sessions, or acupuncture. All of these modalities helped move the grief energy out of his body. Craig described his experience of deep sorrow.

Liesel and I are not putting things in the closet or sweeping them under the rug. It's a challenge to keep the grief in front of us and keep processing it. Our society tends not to look at things that are so difficult. It would be easier to bury the pain, but I know that wouldn't help us heal.

I see emotions as energy in the body. During grief, it's important to express each feeling and move through all its phases until it dissipates. Otherwise, it manifests in the body and causes pain or illness. Kids seem to have a healthy ability to move through their emotions. They feel them, express them, and they're gone. We adults need to be more like kids.

When I went into the deepest grief, I was in complete darkness. I didn't even want to live. Sometimes it would take over my life. It was like a truck ran over me and spilled my guts all over the pavement. For the first couple of years, the grief would come over me in waves. Each time, I had to do something to release all the pain.

Once, I was feeling so compressed I knew I needed to explode. I found myself outside on the patio in a state of rage. Liesel encouraged me to vent my anger by smashing an old picnic table with my bare hands. At first, it seemed like a really bad idea; it went against my Buddhist nature. But she just kept chiding me to do it. Finally I did. Using my bare hands, I destroyed our table, smashing it into a million pieces. It was raining out, and I collapsed in a puddle of water and started wailing.

At first, these dark states were rather terrifying—I didn't feel like it was really me. After a while I came to know, "I'm going through grief, and I'll come home again." Once I understood this, I didn't feel so scared when these waves of deep sorrow came over me. Now, after four years, these dark states come much less often and are less intense.

I don't understand why we human beings have to experience so much grief. Why couldn't I just stay in the glory of communing with my son's spirit? With all my wisdom and spiritual knowledge, I sometimes think I shouldn't have to grieve, but I know that's not the case. The benefit of having a spiritual connection is that when the waves of grief are finished, I'm able to come back to my spiritual viewpoint about life and death. That brings me some comfort.

Signs and Messages From Lucas

After his transition, Lucas sent signs and messages to many in their spiritual community. One friend reported that she walked outside after the ceremony at the hospital and saw a huge rainbow in the sky—even though it wasn't raining. She also saw a hawk flying through the rainbow and felt it was a sign from Lucas.

Penny, Craig's friend who led him to Reiki, kept calling Craig and Liesel to say that Lucas was visiting her regularly and wanted her to pass on his messages. Penny gave Craig and Liesel an hour reading that they recorded. Craig shared some of the highlights of that session.

> *One of the things she told us was that he had been our elder or spiritual teacher in past lives. He chose to incarnate, but then decided not to come through in the physical because he knew he could do more work from the other side. His purpose in coming to our family was to initiate both of us into a deeper level of healing. This has given us the ability to work with our clients at a deeper level.*

Craig continually feels the presence of his spirit son even though they don't engage in conversation—it's a communion that needs no words.

> *I feel our son's energy when I'm doing acupuncture in my office. His presence feels like a thickness around me; there's this warm, heavy sensation, like cotton candy, around my hands. He shows up often—in fact, I call him to come.*

> *Also, Lucas sometimes joins us when we go to church. It's usually when the minister is speaking about something that I need to work on. It seems like my son's spirit alerts me to the next step of my evolutionary journey.*

Craig and Liesel were blessed by the birth of a healthy baby girl about a year after Lucas made his transition. Melia is now three years old and like her parents, is quite sensitive to the higher vibrations of the spirit world. Craig explained.

> *Melia mentions Lucas several times a week. She's talked about him from the time she could use words. It seems he's very much a part of her everyday life. Sometimes it's just a comment like, "My brother is here." One day she casually announced, "Daddy, my brother is in the shower. Can you open the door for him?"*

Craig commented that, surprisingly, Melia's birth demanded Liesel and he deal with another level of grief about Lucas because each day with the new baby showed them what they had missed with their son.

A Higher Purpose

Craig explained how his experience with their precious infant became a catalyst for his own soul growth and was excited to be able to see the higher purpose.

The birth and death of our son seems to have great purpose; however, we don't understand it all yet because much of that purpose is still unfolding. It's been the biggest turning point in our lives. Liesel and I are so much closer now. His birth and death lifted each of us onto our life's path. We were both infused with a spiritual energy that expanded us and allowed us to relate to others on a higher level. We now have so much more compassion for the suffering of others.

I totally believe that before coming to earth, Lucas, Liesel, and I all made a soul agreement that he would come and be our teacher. I'm still discovering some of the soul lessons I'm here to learn.

My experience with our son expanded my consciousness. You might say I awakened to a much deeper level. Spirit is no longer just a mental concept. And it's so much more than the fleeting glimpses I used to experience while doing yoga or breath work. Without using any words, Lucas taught me that Spirit is pure light, joy, love, and bliss.

Being with the spirit of our son for those two weeks was an initiation into the work we are here to do on the planet. It was one of the reasons for the whole experience. Before Lucas, I didn't have as great an ability to hold space for clients who were going through a deep process. I could stay present with them, but I couldn't relate to their intense suffering. Now, after my experience with Lucas, I can be present at the deepest level for anything my clients are going through.

Lucas has a Buddha-like energy—his presence inspires deep transformation and healing. We witnessed Lucas spark so many miraculous healings in our spiritual community. It was amazing! I sometimes remember the swami's prediction, "This child that's coming to you is going to be very pious and do great things for the planet." I trust this is true, and one of those great things is to assist in raising the consciousness of the planet. His spirit is pure love, and his energetic presence invites people into that same state. I believe this is his purpose.

Points to Ponder

In this story, Craig moves back and forth, using his soul eyes and his human eyes to view his son's transition to the other side—both perspectives are real for him at different times. His healing journey is a model for moving through devastating grief and integrating both the human and the divine experience.

Together, Craig and Liesel demonstrate "a new way to experience death," and they give this precious gift to their extended family members, all the people in their healing community, and now to you, the reader. Their blissful experiences with the spirit of their beloved infant demonstrate, once again, *there is no death.* For several weeks, they are able to raise their vibration and become part of the Oneness that now surrounds their precious child. They are blessed to have more than a little glimpse of heaven—it is more like a near-death experience that continues for weeks. *Can you imagine the spirit of your infant also existing in this place of Oneness? Can you also imagine being uplifted and having your own little glimpse of heaven?* Craig and Liesel show us that, indeed, this is a viable possibility.

In *Connected for All Time: Book One*, I presented this Radiant Heart Healing premise: *The key to healing after loss is to release the grief energy and then fill your heart with the energy of love.* Craig demonstrates the effectiveness of this method. He has a deep understanding of painful emotions as energy that needs to move through the body and be discharged. We see that he makes many powerful choices for releasing his devastating pain—allowing himself to cry or even wail at times, smashing a picnic table to vent his anger, and using many forms of bodywork to move the heavy energy of grief through his system. At the same time, he continually fills his heart with the energy of love from his spirit son, his wife, and the many healers in their spiritual community. Here, like all the other stories in this book, we see a spirit baby filling a grieving parent's heart with deep soul love. In doing so, Lucas brings powerful medicine to his father—just like the Inca spirit babies described to me by Wachan, the medicine man I met at Bell Rock in Sedona, Arizona.

Craig and Liesel's spiritual community is a compelling force in this story. This powerful spirit named Lucas sends messages to many in their healing network throughout his entire journey—while in the womb, on life support, and again after his transition to the other side. It's no accident that people spontaneously show up at the hospital to witness and honor his transition. It's one of those synchronistic events orchestrated by Spirit. *Craig and Liesel's experience with Lucas is a community experience, and everyone involved is raised to a higher level of consciousness. And, as has been stated previously in this book, this is the most important spiritual growth anyone can accomplish.*

Think about yourself, your beloved spirit baby, and all the people directly or indirectly connected to you—they are your community. *What are you learning as you heal? Are you growing spiritually and embracing more wisdom? Are you expanding your capacity to share love? How has your baby's birth and death effected others in your community? Who are the angels in human form who have lifted you up during your time of grief? As you heal, are you generating more love so others in your community are also uplifted?*

It is our soul's very nature to keep learning, growing, embracing more wisdom, and expanding our capacity to share love. This is a universal purpose of every soul who comes to earth. It is especially true for anyone who needs to overcome the tragedy of losing a beloved baby.

CHAPTER TEN

Conclusion

At first glance, this book appears to be a collection of stories about healing grief after the tragedy of miscarriage or infant death. However, when you look deeper, you'll find it's really a book about *spiritual awakening and the evolution of human consciousness*. This focus on spiritual development is absolutely necessary because awakening to Spirit is the only way to heal the deep soul wound caused by the death of a beloved baby. Those who have been able to remember their baby with love instead of pain are the ones who have come to realize who they really are. And who are you really? You are a magnificent, powerful soul who has come to earth to evolve and learn the lessons of love. And who is your beloved baby really? He or she is also a powerful soul who came to earth for a short time and chose your family to accomplish some sacred purpose.

Without a doubt the death of every baby has meaning and purpose. Furthermore, Spirit connected me with story after story, showing that *whenever an infant dies, there is a sacred pre-birth plan developed at the soul level for both the death of this infant and the spiritual evolution of the family as they heal their grief.* Our souls know the truth about this divine plan, but at the human level we have forgotten. All of these stories invite us to remember.

After the loss of an infant I believe the souls of all grieving family members call for them to awaken spiritually and become conscious of this pre-birth plan. At this time in our human evolution only a few can hear the call of their souls. However, we live at a time of great spiritual awakening on planet earth—2012 is almost upon us. As more and more people evolve to higher levels of consciousness, we can expect that they too will see the death of a baby (as well as other loved ones) from both the human and spiritual viewpoints. When this occurs, I anticipate a major shift in mass consciousness about life, death, life after death, funeral services, and healing grief. Then our whole society will begin to deal with these issues in a more enlightened way. All of the people who shared their stories in *Connected for All Time: Book One* and *Book Two* are here on earth to make this shift happen. Indeed, it is an important part of their soul purpose.

A part of my soul purpose has also been fulfilled in writing these books that provide a new model for healing grief. As mass consciousness evolves and humankind becomes more enlightened, this model will be more and more accepted and seen as the natural way to transform grief. *Can you imagine a time when people are so spiritually awake that the bliss of Oneness becomes a common experience after the death of a loved one?* This is my hope for humanity. These Spirit-guided books are part of a bigger plan to facilitate a major shift in consciousness so that the sting of death is extinguished, and we all come to know this truth: *Love is eternal and the spirits of our loved ones exist in the bliss of Oneness. And—we are connected for all time.*

Acknowledgements

There are so many who have gifted me with their inspiration, guidance, and support so this book could become a reality. First, I'd like to acknowledge the assistance from Spirit: all the spirits of the babies in this book, as well as my own guides and angels, who worked with me from beginning to end. Throughout the writing journey I felt as if I had a "baby on my shoulder" giving me inspiration and guidance. Second, I'd like to thank all the mothers, fathers, siblings, aunts, and grandparents who had the courage to share their precious stories of communication from a beloved spirit baby. Their stories are the heart of *Connected for All Time: Book One* and *Book Two*.

The artwork on the cover is entitled *Angels' Lullaby* and was created by Carolyn Utigard Thomas (www.utigard.com). I'll always remember the spark of joy in my heart when I found this picture of an angel holding a baby. I knew in the moment that the spirit babies had guided me to the perfect image for this book. I want to extend my thanks to Carolyn for allowing me to use this wonderful artwork. Connie Kouba of Kouba Graphics Inc. (www.koubagraphics.com) designed the beautiful cover and did the typesetting for the manuscript. She was a joy to work with and her artistic design abilities brought this project to a delightful conclusion.

This book evolved with the assistance of numerous editors over a period of ten years. My heartfelt thanks to Judith Howard for her countless hours spent editing and formatting this work. Her assistance gave me the creative freedom to write without worrying about the details of grammar, punctuation, and formatting. I also want to thank these editors who contributed to this project at various times: Jan Alligretti, Cynthia Richmond, Jane Francis, Penny Hiernu, Ann Ramage, and Leah Janeczko.

I wish to acknowledge Roy Waite, my mentor and first spiritual teacher. He taught me that spirit communication is real and that, indeed, spirit babies can send messages to their family members here on earth. Thank you also to the numerous healers, psychics, and spiritual mediums who contributed metaphysical insights from their readings: Akeeya, Barbara Norman, Chief Joseph, Sandra Cheek, Carol Tunney, Carol Mann, Jane Francis, Robert Peace, Linda Eastburn, and Wachan, the Inca medicine man.

Finally, I'd like to thank my husband, Dr. Jerry Wesch, for his never-ending support as I fulfilled the call of Spirit to write this book. It's such a joy to have his love and encouragement.

Grief Resources

The organizations listed below provide support and resources for families grieving the loss of a child. In addition, you may want to refer to my website (www.connectedforalltime.com) for a list of spiritual mediums and their contact information.

Bereaved Parents of the USA
Park Forest, Illinois
www.bereavedparents.org

The Compassionate Friends
Oakbrook, Illinois
www.compassionatefriends.org

Forever Family Foundation
Oceanside, New York
www.foreverfamilyfoundation.com

Good Grief Center for Bereavement Support
Pittsburgh, Pennsylvania
www.goodgriefcenter.com

Pregnancy Loss and Infant Death Alliance (PLIDA)
Parker, Colorado
www.plida.org

SHARE Pregnancy and Infant Loss Support
Charles, Missouri
www.nationalshare.org

SIDS Alliance
Baltimore, Maryland
www.sidsalliance.org

National Spiritualist Association of Churches
Lily Dale, New York
www.nsac.org
Provides information about mediums and spiritualist churches

Prayer Wave for After-Death Communication
www.christineduminiak.com
Internet grief support and prayer website
Their mission is to pray for others desiring to receive after-death communication